50 Beds:
Innovations in Design and Materials

5O BEDS

Innovations in Design and Materials

Mel Byars

Introduction by
Brice d'Antras

Research by
Cinzia Anguissola d'Altoé
Brice d'Antras

Technical drawings by
Marvin Klein

A RotoVision Book

PRO DESIGN SERIES

Published by RotoVision SA
Rue du Bugnon, 7
CH-1299 Crans-Près-Céligny
Switzerland

RotoVision SA
Sales & Production Office
Sheridan House
112/116A Western Road
Hove BN3 IDD, U.K.
Tel: +44 (0)1273 7272 68
Fax: +44 (0)1273 7272 69
E-mail: sales@rotovision.com
Website: www.rotovision.com

Distributed to the trade in the United States by
Watson-Guptill Publications
770 Broadway
8th Floor
New York, NY 10003-9595
U.S.A.

Copyright © 2000 Mel Byars

ISBN 2-88046-449-8

This book was written, designed, and
produced by Mel Byars.

Printed in Singapore
Production and separations in
Singapore by ProVision Pte. Ltd.
Tel: +65 334 7720
Fax: +65 334 7721

50 Chairs: Innovations in Design and Materials
by Mel Byars with an Introduction by Alexander von Vegesack

50 Tables: Innovations in Design and Materials
by Mel Byars with an Introduction by Sylvain Dubuisson

50 Lights: Innovations in Design and Materials
by Mel Byars with an Introduction by Paola Antonelli

50 Products: Innovations in Design and Materials
by Mel Byars with an Introduction by David Revere McFadden

50 Sports Wares: Innovations in Design and Materials
by Mel Byars with an Introduction by Aaron Betsky

50 Beds: Innovations in Design and Materials
by Mel Byars with an Introduction by Brice d'Antras

Contents

Introduction

The Bed: A Shared Intimacy

The bed is the ultimate shrine to contemporary intimacy. Designed as a place of rest and pleasure for a single person or a couple, in the last decade or so it has been stripped of most of the attributes that previously gave it a social, even cultural, role. Forsaking the canopy, hangings, and wooden bedposts, today's bed is more like a divan that has been fitted with a headboard. In this contemporary version, it has retained the techniques of its construction; its marks of status have remained discreet, and it has been made safe by a reassuring, unthreatening simplicity, at the extremes of a rigorous stylistic absence of ornament. It would, however, be hasty to reduce it to nothing more than a parallelepiped, a platform for sleeping or for sex.

Mel Byars, as a design psychoanalyst, is interested in the bed as an object more repressed than liberated by functionalist imperatives. This selection of 50 beds expresses the technical, formalist, theatrical, humorous, and even erotic fantasies of the kind of richly sensuous bedding that the Protestant prurience in modern design has mostly repressed.

In contrast to previous centuries, the bedroom and the bed have relinquished the terrain that represents a social role. Power is no longer exercised through a sovereign's ceremonial levee and his going-to-bed, a politically federating ritual, as in the 18th century. And the bedroom is no longer the place for literary battles. Today individuals' demands have replaced those of the group's well-being, or the collective rules of deportment. The bed no longer exists to support a public pose but rather to provide comfort for the body. Western societies, by building their progress on the satisfaction of individual needs, have developed a concept of intimacy like no other society before. This phenomenon has become one of the cardinal virtues of our age. A succession of evermore tightly sealed doors protects, isolates some say, the bed of the contemporary citizen-consumer from the street. Although, largely liberated from the imperatives of a public image, intimacy has not, paradoxically, eliminated the signs that codify the rules of collective behavior. The enormous cultural significance of the bed—a place important not only for love, birth, and death but also for dreams and nightmares—prevents its being reduced to pure function, or only a place of horizontal rest.

The shape of the bed is a kind of collective regulation of individual behavior that is being insistently proposed by society and accepted with eagerness. In their intimacy, individuals need to feel secure, to feel part of the group through the sharing of collective values, even by those who govern their private behavior. The bed reflects the image perceived as being important to the society of its users.

Invariably, a new-born baby's cot is returned to the idea of innocence through the choice of colors like blue and pink—always pastel or white—and is displayed with excessive emotion through the baroque over-abundance of curves, fancy linens, lace, and drapes. The cot that Peter Keller designed at the Bauhaus in 1922, consisting of circles, triangles, squares, and in primary colors, was and is still a pure and sterile academic fiction. The physiological necessities of nutrition and defecation, essential to infants, are ignored. Although equipment is necessary to ensure the health or medication of the baby, the essentials are hidden in order to cause as little disruption as possible to the display of that contemporary icon, the baby.

The teenage boy finds himself with a single bed, bare of decorative features and any encouragement of pleasure. He is in a period of learning the male rules of life. His sexuality, essentially solitary, can be neither evoked nor, still less, displayed. One finds the same repugnance for decorative emotion—a watered-down translation of the adult's sentimental and sexual emotion—in communal premises like school and military dormitories and prison cells.

The matrimonial bed is a statement of the commitment and stability of the institution of coupledom. A bed or mattress on the floor is reserved for the young or those on the margins of society. It represents a place for only rest or pleasure, without responsibility for the social cohesion of the group. Yet the matrimonial bed is raised on legs, a gesture that transforms it into a kind of elongated throne, symbolizing the perpetuation of the group and the transmission of its values. Casters are either banned or hidden. Despite several attempts, the addition of wheels has remained incompatible with the notion of conjugal stability. The headboard, essentially a decorative addition, ennobles the marriage bed by imbuing it with symbolic uprightness. A successor to the canopy, the headboard is a vestige of the bed's ancestry.

With the curiosity of an entomologist and always with humor and irony, Mel Byars has ventured here in this volume into the contemporary setting of the bed. Far from offering solutions, he proposes highly original forms that make us question our human and social behavior and our relationship with technology and pleasure. A futurologist, he prefigures the many focal points of tomorrow by casting light on the margins of today.

Brice d'Antras
Professor
École supérieure d'art et de design
Reims, France

Foreword

Sweet Dreams

50 Beds is the last volume of six in the Pro-Design series published by RotoVision. And, with its publication, you might say that we are putting the series to bed.

While some of the other subjects covered in the group—like chairs, lights, and sports equipment—are mainly basic industrial-design categories, beds are a whole other animal. By the very nature of how many of us live, beds today must frequently serve multiple purposes, maybe some you have never thought about, not just sleeping, resting, watching television, or having sex. For instance, at home I do all my non-computer work and eat every meal in bed.

You will find many examples here that serve multiple purposes—for example, beds that morph into desks or into sofas. One of them even unfolds from a sofa into bunk beds (pages 118–20), but you must see the steps of the transformation to believe it. It's like watching a chrysalid become an insect. And there are others that you purchase flat or disassembled and then assemble yourself (pages 38–41, 48–50, 124–31).

Of the standard-configuration types (essentially a platform on legs), there are beds built to offer a certain amount of flexibility (pages 22–25, 40–41, 48–50). Another standard bed type (pages 20–21) is operated by a memory-retaining remote-controlled motor that changes the angles of the mattress platform, and the energy-saving motor closes down when not being used.

And, true to the books in Pro-Design series, there are beds that question the very definition of "bed" or "chaise longue." In other words, they are far from ordinary and rather bizarre. One unusual example incorporates a motor into what looks like a large blue tongue that replicates the sensations produced by an ocean wave. Still another example—a plastic form that looks like a real wave caught at mid-break—may be more a piece of art than a utilitarian object; nevertheless, it's a chaise longue.

And, concerning chaise longues, there is a chapter here devoted to them because they are more or less—maybe less—a type of bed, objects for repose, or surfaces on which you rest for a shorter time than beds.

Since there are 50 beds here, the numerous examples cover the gamut of possibilities—from futons on a platform and inflatable units to hide-aways and devices with intricate mechanics. Many include the kinds of amazing high-tech materials we now take for granted and are made with cutting-edge production processes that are available these days to a wider range of small manufacturers.

No book on beds would be complete without cribs, cradles, and at least one dog bed. And they are all here.

There are cribs in new wood, used wood, cardboard, felt, and even a synthetic material known as Madéron, a plastic made from almond shells. And the *japonisme* version of a dog bed shown here is obviously for highly pampered pooches because the cushion is upholstered in silk. The other 14 versions of this particular canine sleeping-couch include Louis XIII and XVI, Biedermier, Arabic, Secessionist, Art Déco, and Roman-temple motifs. All of this luxury is no doubt for the sole gratification of the owners and not for their pups.

The problem with compiling the material for this book has been an ongoing one with all the books in the Pro-Design series: acquiring supplementary drawings, deconstructed images, and in-production pictures—not just nice product photographs by professional photographers. The acquisition was often thwarted due to several daunting factors, including lackadaisical, uncooperative, disinterested, or absent-minded designers and manufacturers.

Fortunately, the primary people—Brice d'Antras in Paris and Cinzia Anguissola d'Altoá in Milan—who have helped me with most of the books in the series have been indefatigable and generous. They made *50 Beds* possible. Their contribution helped me to realize my quest toward providing examples from around the globe. In the end, the work here—while not truly international—was furnished to us by designers who immigrated from, are natives of, or have worked in a dozen countries: Argentina, Czech Republic, Denmark, Germany, the Netherlands, Russia, Spain, Sweden, Switzerland, the United Kingdom, and the U.S.A., including from where most of the designers and manufacturers reside—France and Italy.

So, to the editorial and production staff of the publisher RotoVision, the printer ProVision, the designers, the manufacturers, the photographers, Brice, Cinzia, and all others who were part of making *50 Beds* happen, thank you and may you have sweet dreams.

Mel Byars
New York City

50 Beds:
Innovations in Design and Materials

Standard Configurations

Lit-bibliothèque (Bed-Bookcase)

Designer: Eric Benqué (French)
Manufacturer: Néotù, Paris, France
Date of design: 1999

The bent-plywood base of this bed serves as both base and legs. The space between the mattress platform and the base accommodates the placement of books for easy access, since many of us read in bed. The double-layer headboard also has an inner space where magazines and newspapers can be kept.

Solid sycamore spacers, rabbeted crosswise into the platform and base.

Five-ply wood (inner layers in poplar; veneer in ashwood).

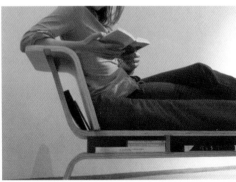

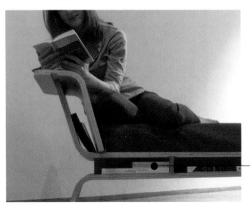

The movable double headboard accommodates newspapers and magazines in the space between.

Books kept beneath the mattress are handy.

Bed

Designer: Jeffrey Bernett (American)
Manufacturer: Cappellini S.p.A., Arosio
(CO), Italy
Date of design: 1997

Unadorned, like much of this designer's
work, the bed here in sheet aluminum
is congruent with a range of seating he
designed for the same manufacturer.
Models are available in brushed or
painted aluminum. The simple assembly
is realized through the use of exposed
screws.

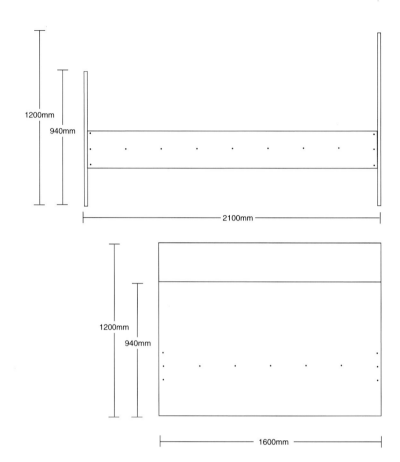

Aluminum sheets: brushed (below) or
painted in a range of bright colors (right).

Super Cad bed

Designers: Treca design staff
Manufacturer: Treca, Issy-les-Moulineaux,
France
Date of design: 1996

The Super Cad is able to assume five positions
which have been modeled on the morphology
of the body. All the functions are controlled
separately. The four independent electric
motors are silent and automatically in the "off"
mode when not in use.

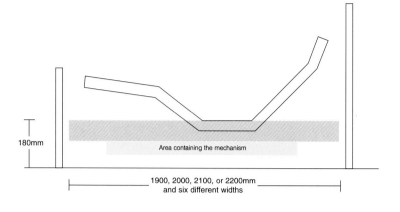

180mm

Area containing the mechanism

1900, 2000, 2100, or 2200mm
and six different widths

Two braided endstops (from
1300–1400mm), with a ticking
cover, ensure that the mattress
remains in perfect position.

Steel main frame.

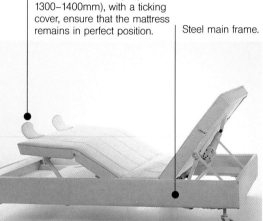

The entire bed surface draws backward to remain near the bed-
head, when the head rest and upper body are raised.

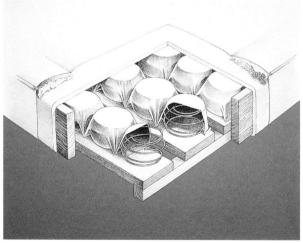

The brushed-aluminum or imitation-wood-finished high-frequency
remote control provides these incremental instructions:

Raise headrest.	Raise legs.	Return to horizontal.
Lower headrest.	Lower legs.	Recall of memorized positions.
Raise upper body.	Raise incline.	Possible individual functions.
Lower upper body.	Lower incline.	

The pocket springs offer independent action and, purportedly,
comfort. High-quality steel provides elasticity.

Bilove bed

Designers: Christopher Burtscher (Austrian) and
Patrizia Bertolini (Italian)
Manufacturer: Malofancon S.n.c., Malo (VI), Italy
Date of design: 1993

The finish on this bed is composed of ecologically
friendly oils and waxes that are applied hot with a
spray gun and set with Scotch Brite. The construction
is very simple—absent of screws and metal parts—and
easy to assemble and transport. The raked angle of
the slats and the elastomer pad produce a high
degree of elasticity.

Acute-angle slats of the platform cantilever beyond the legs.

Elastomer pad offers bounce to the platform.

No metal parts or screws are necessary for assembly; instead, a C.E.E.-approved vinyl resin is used.

All parts are bio-ecologically finished solid beechwood.

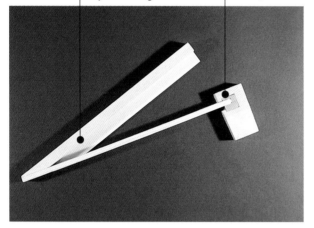

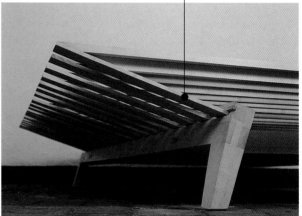

Bilove bed

Optional upholstered headboard or removable pillows (shown here) are available.

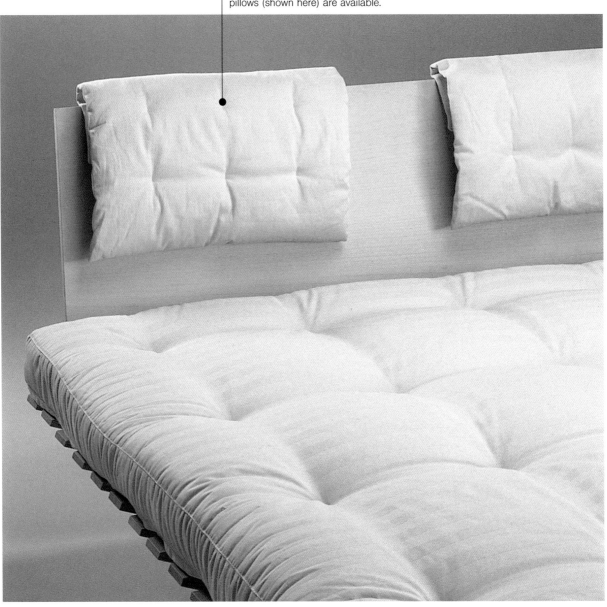

The platform may be used without a headboard.

Bedfordshire bed

Designer: Andrew Stafford (British)
Manufacturer: Stafford, London, United Kingdom
Date of design: 1994

The design of this bed was developed over a period of four years and then, from 1998, by the designer's own firm in England. It is available with a single or double headboard that is fixed or pivotable at any angle. All edges are rounded for protection from bumps and scrapes.

Most popular length/width/height here (but available in others, depending on the country).

1550mm

800mm

2100mm

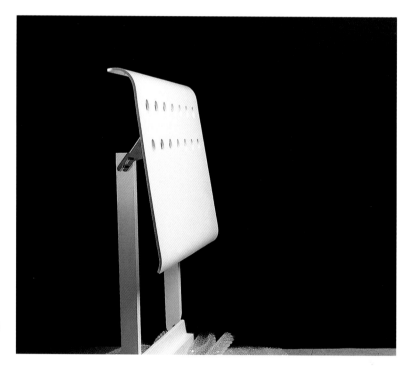

Detail of the headrest's stainless-steel mechanism that offers positioning at any angle.

5

Bedfordshire bed

One of the versions built during the extended history of the bed's development.

Molded plywood with
adjustable stainless-
steel mechanism.

Sprung laminat-
ed beechwood
slats support
the mattress.

Fully locking
chromatized-zinc
casters with
rubber treads, or
turned maplewood
or American
walnut legs.

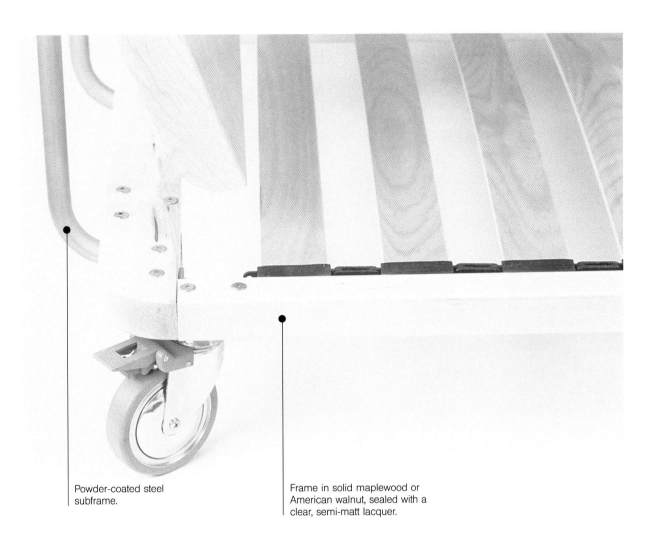

Powder-coated steel
subframe.

Frame in solid maplewood or
American walnut, sealed with a
clear, semi-matt lacquer.

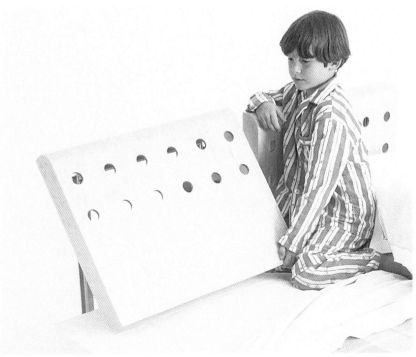

Mobilier en ligne/ligne de mobilier (furniture in line/line of furniture)

Designer: Frédéric Ruyant (French)
Manufacturer: prototype by Société Ufacto, Montreuil, France, funded by V.I.A., Paris
Date of design: 2000

This group of furniture—arranged as single pieces or in a single line, as shown here—offers an alternative to the kind of suites newlyweds frequently purchase from stores that cater to the homologous public. However, this suite is obviously intended to furnish a single person's apartment. The material used for construction is a sandwich of MDF (medium-density-fiber) board.

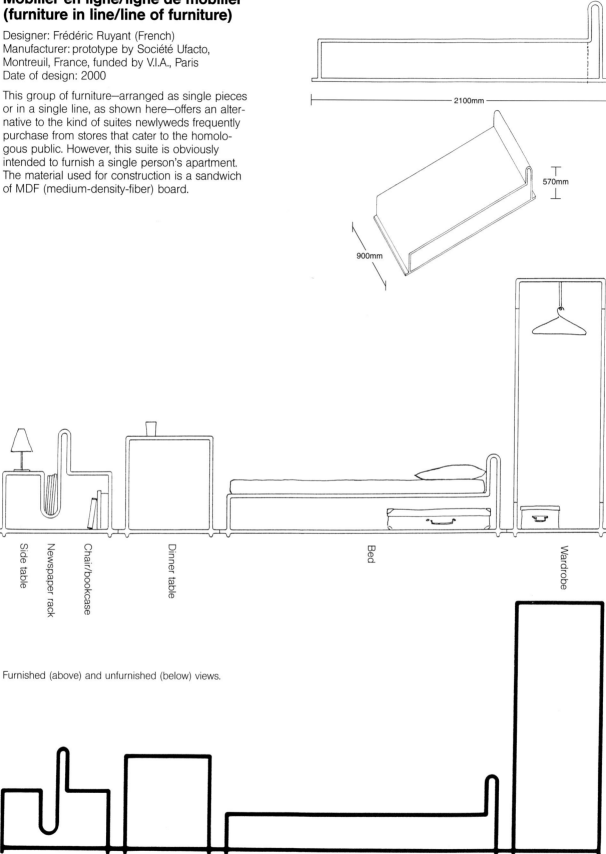

2100mm

570mm

900mm

Side table

Newspaper rack

Chair/bookcase

Dinner table

Bed

Wardrobe

Furnished (above) and unfurnished (below) views.

Palazzo Strozzi bed

Designer: Borek Sípek (Czech)
Manufacturer: Studio Sípek, Amsterdam,
the Netherlands
Date of design: 1991

This bed is a peculiar amalgamation of both inexpensive and luxurious materials. A native of the former Czechoslovakia, a place known for its fine mouth-blown glass, the designer is particularly fond of this material that he uses in one example here. These three *mises en scène* are clearly fantasies conjured from the mind of Sípek rather than practical bedroom settings.

Mouth-blown glass finials.

Hand-painted posts. (See facing page.)

The scene below features a bed with hand-painted posts and linen bed sheets, a pillow, and canopy. The platform is unfinished wood.

7

Palazzo Strozzi bed

The bed here in a different setting is
a more expanded interpretation of
the other three.

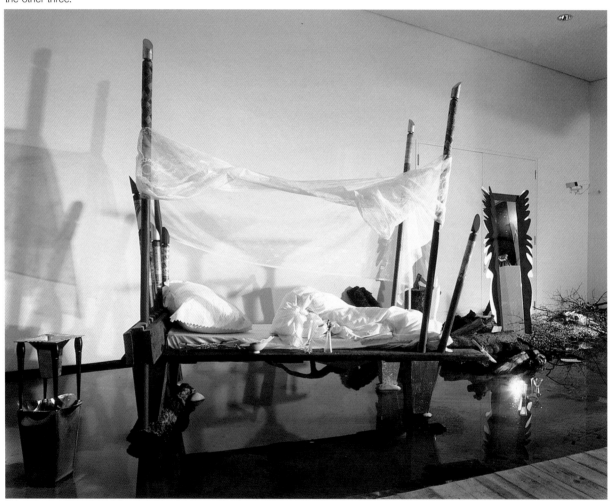

Platforms

8

Assis Lang® bed

Designer: Arthur Huser and Christof Anliker
(both Swiss)
Manufacturer: the designers
Date of design: 1999

This bed was a competition winner in a contest
for furniture and other interior products that
specifically exploited the use of Corian, the
DuPont material that was introduced in 1967.
However, this particular bed or chaise longue
can easily be produced in natural plywood.

Nine pairs
of wheels (10
mm high)
with rubber
treads are
placed at
every other
slit and
attached with
screws, the
only fasten-
ers used.

The slits are
machine-
sawn and
wheel holes
machine-
drilled.

600mm

1800mm

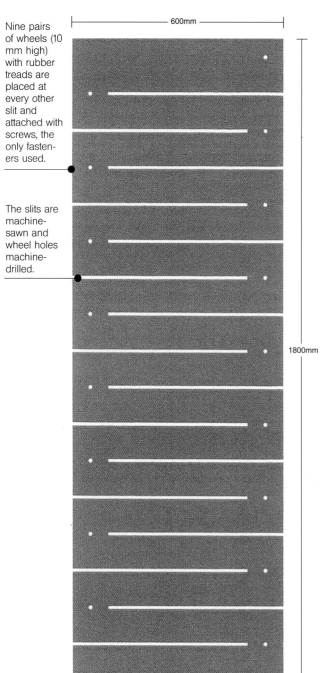

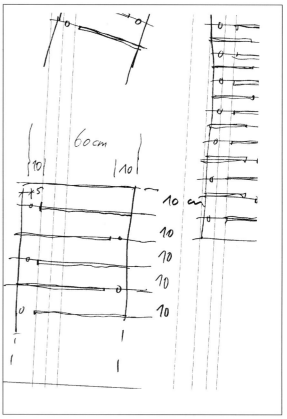

Two of the drawings by the designers.

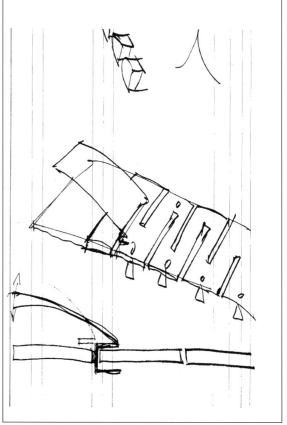

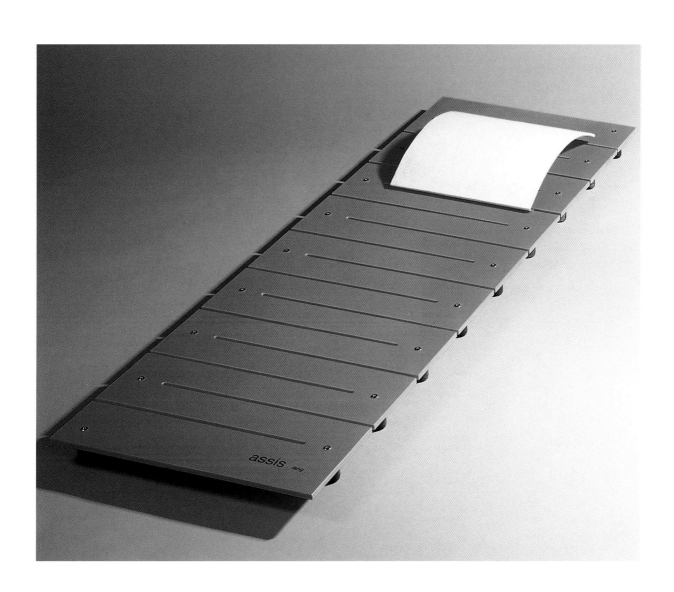

9

Gravitá (Gravity) bed

Designer: Paola Balderacchi (Italian)
Manufacturer: Paola Balderacchi—Tupa®,
Milano, Italy
Date of design: 1990

To describe this bed, the designer offers
this theorem from Leonardo: "Lightness and
heaviness are both the mother and daugh-
ter of each other." The simple idea here is
composed of essentially two shaped side
pieces that are held in place by dovetailed
stave supports. The elements are held
together by gravity, thus eliminating the
necessity for glue or metal fasteners.

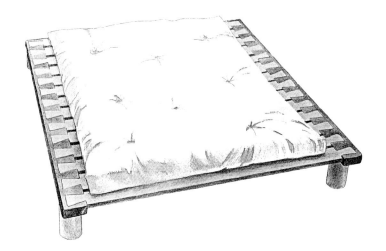

13 traditionally dove-
tailed staves that sup-
port the mattress hold
the unit taut.

Beechwood has been
selected from controlled
forests. All wood was
chosen because it
decreases the energy
necessary for its finishing,
thermal conductivity, and
static electricity. It also
offers resilience, easy
repair, recycling, and
modification, and is
pleasant to touch, smell,
and see.

Sottiletto (Thin Bed)

Designers: Christof Burtscher (Austrian) and
Patrizia Bertolini (Italian)
Manufacturer: Horm S.r.l, Milano, Italy
Date of design: 1997

The first version of the platform of this bed featured a single, long cross bar that ran between
the slats and down the center. But it was difficult
to weave the bar over and under the slats, and
also it was not particularly flexible. Therefore,
individual plastic spacers were developed to be
placed at each opening.

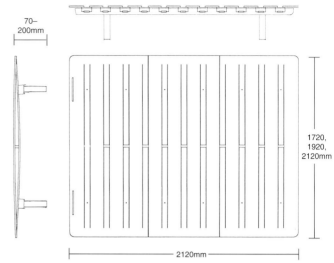

70–
200mm

1720,
1920,
2120mm

2120mm

Transparent methyl methacrylate
spacers are used as separators at
every opening.

Produced in beechwood.
four finishes are available: natural,
mocha, cherry, and white.

First version (right) illustrates
the less-effective cross bar
down the center.

The slats are 12mm thick. They
would work as well in a 9mm
thickness, but 12mm creates a
greater sense of strength in
customers' minds.

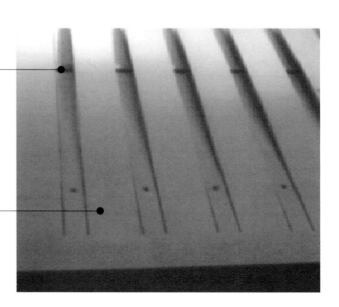

Scherenbett (Folding Bed) No. 990

Designer: Benjamin Thut
Manufacturer: Thut Möbel AG, Möriken, Switzerland
Date of design: 1995

The Thut firm produces a small range of cabinets and beds. The bed frame here is a configuration of wooden slats that can be adjusted in increments from 940mm to 1940mm wide, to accommodate mattress sizes from single to double.

Attached
table
Ø400mm

214–223mm

940–1940mm

A fold-arm halogen lighting figure is integrated into the platform.

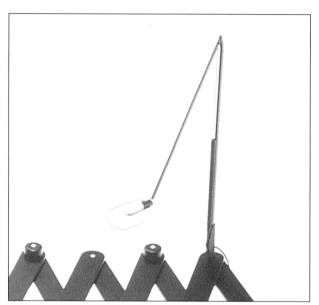

The platform is shown here in its narrowest folded position.

The beechwood slats are available painted black or left natural.

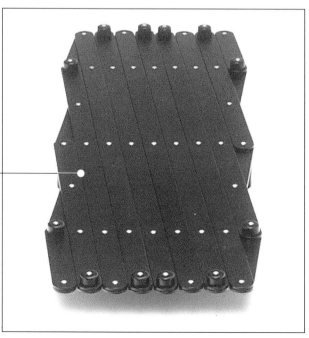

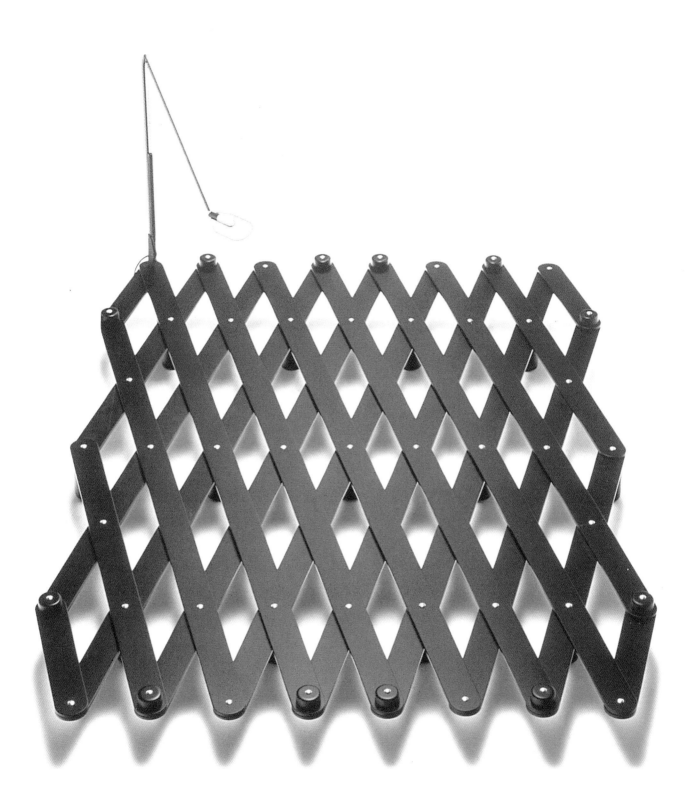

12

Lit clos

Designer: Erwan Bouroullec (French)
Manufacturer: original prototype by Les
Ateliers des Arques in 1997; Cappellini S.p.A.,
Arosio (CO), Italy from 2000
Date of design: 1997

The source for this design is far more traditional than it may appear. The form is remi-
niscent of the early bed units that were built
into a corner area and closed off by a door
or curtain for privacy and warmth. These
beds were often a part of a public area in a
French farmhouse. However, the Bouroullec
bed is more like a treehouse.

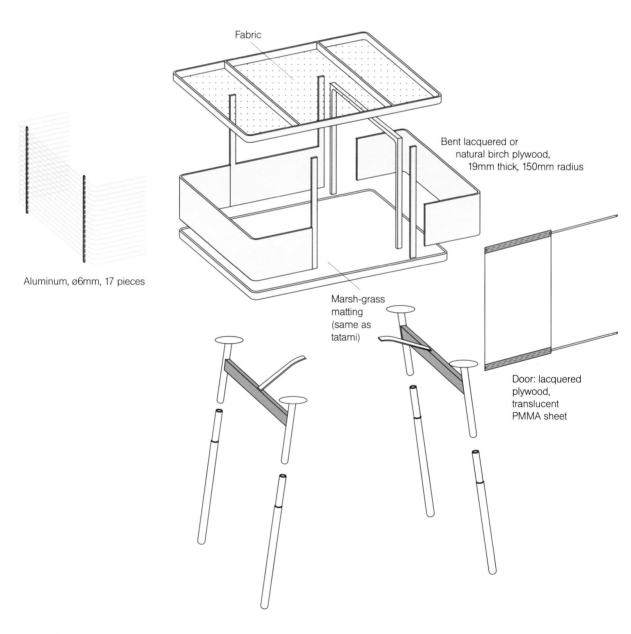

Fabric

Bent lacquered or
natural birch plywood,
19mm thick, 150mm radius

Aluminum, ø6mm, 17 pieces

Marsh-grass
matting
(same as
tatami)

Door: lacquered
plywood,
translucent
PMMA sheet

Lit clos

Disks at the tops of the painted steel legs are attached to the underside of the sleeping cabinet.

Nylon glides are inserted
into the ends of the legs.

A view of the entry opening.
Aluminum-rod screen at left.

Aluminum track on
which the door slides.

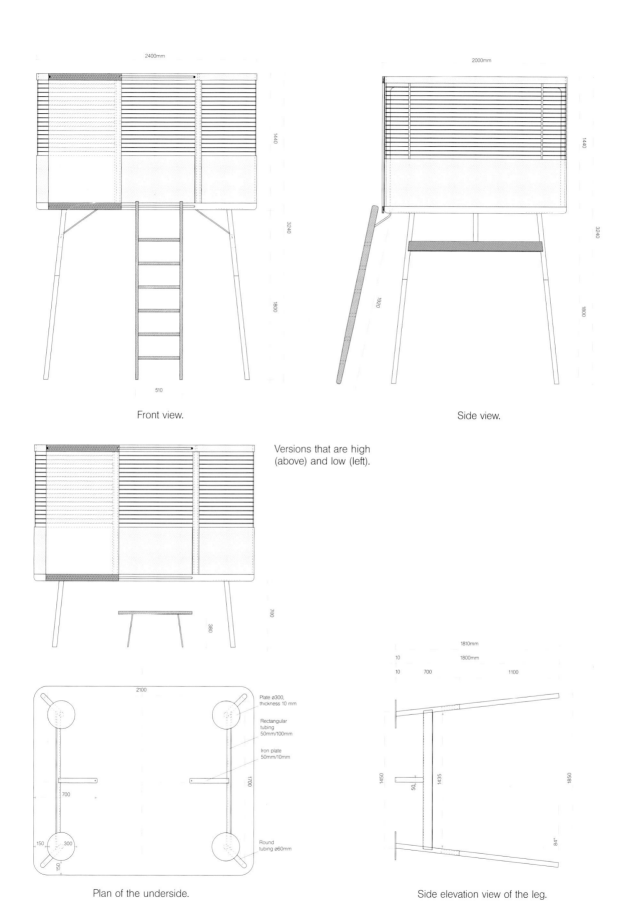

2400mm

1440

3240

1800

510

Front view.

2000mm

1440

3240

1920

1800

Side view.

Versions that are high
(above) and low (left).

700

380

Plan of the underside.

2100

1700

700

150   300

150

Plate ø300,
thickness 10 mm

Rectangular
tubing
50mm/100mm

Iron plate
50mm/10mm

Round
tubing ø60mm

1810mm
10   1800mm
10   700   1100

1450

50

1435

1850

84°

Side elevation view of the leg.

Canoa (Canoe)

Designers: Paolo Cogliati and Luigi Barba (both Italian)
Manufacturer: Totem Italia, Milano (MI), Italy
Date of design: 1998

The stability and construction of this bed depends on the user. Building it may be complicated but requires no special know-how. Each of the elements has specific functional characteristics, and no glue, tools, nails, or other metallic or rubber parts are required for assembly. The kit includes all the necessary plywood pieces, assembly instructions, and a bottle of oil to finish the surfaces. The Canoa is one piece of furniture in a range that includes chests, a chair, crib, bookcase, and lighting fixtures.

No adhesives or fasteners are used in the bed's construction. Inexpensive to ship in its deconstructed form, the bed is easy to store, if necessary.

6mm-thick beech plywood pieces are assembled by the end user.

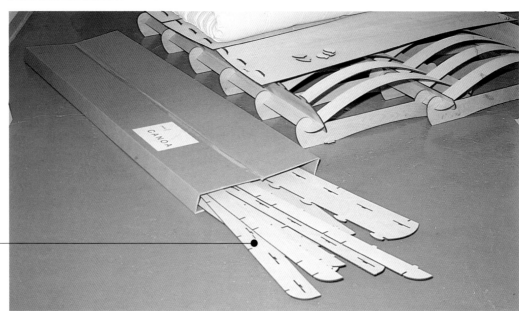

Canoa (Canoe)

The plywood pieces are laser-cut and held together by constant tension. Because of the tensioning system, each bed is flexible, strong, lightweight, solid and stable.

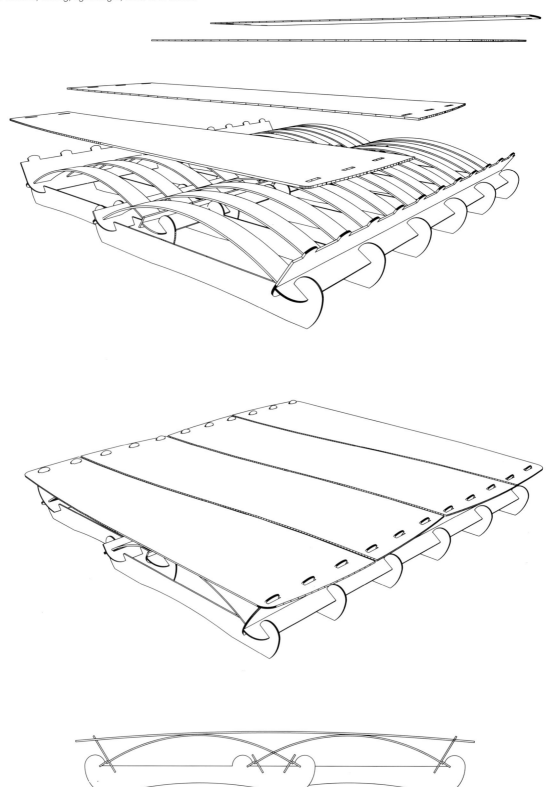

14

Studio daybed/bench

Designer: Konstantin Grcic (German)
Manufacturer: Cappellini S.p.A., Arosio
(CO), Italy
Date of design: 1994

The development of this daybed or
bench—painted white or black—was
based on the designer's habit of dozing
horizontally for 10–15 minutes in his
"studio" (thus, the name) after lunch.
The structure combines round and
square tubing.

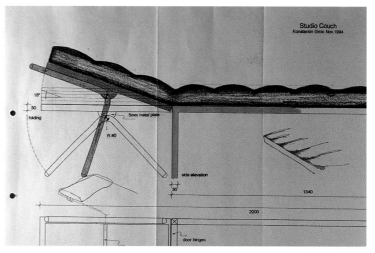

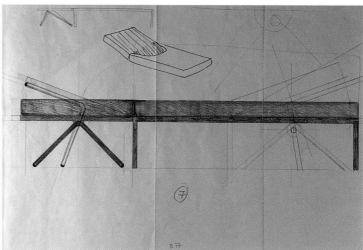

The designer's drawings. Dimensions (flat) are 2000mm wide
x 700mm deep x 350mm high.

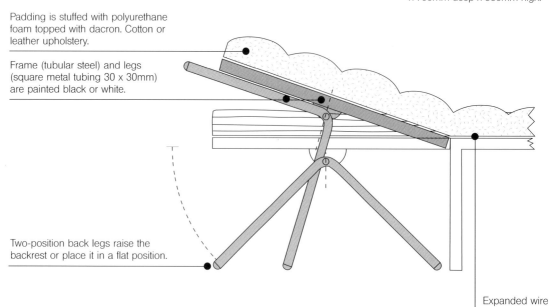

Padding is stuffed with polyurethane
foam topped with dacron. Cotton or
leather upholstery.

Frame (tubular steel) and legs
(square metal tubing 30 x 30mm)
are painted black or white.

Two-position back legs raise the
backrest or place it in a flat position.

Expanded wire
mesh with the metal
frame, beneath the
cushion.

15

Moods bed/chaise/chair

Designer: Jean-Marc Gady (French)
Manufacturer: prototype by Cintrage
Mécanique, Société Cockpit, Société Oris
Decoration, and Société Bois Carbonne
Design (BCD), all France, funded by
V.I.A., Paris
Date of design: 1999

This daybed is a platform with an adjustable
back that can be articulated in several
positions facilitated by an integrated track
system. A user may sit upright as on a side
chair, recline as on a chaise longue, or lie
down as on a daybed. The designer claims
that the severity and simplicity of dormitory
beds was the source of his inspiration,
though Moods is far more glamorous and
certainly more comfortable.

The special track
(shown here from both
sides) is installed
under the seat and
makes the sliding of
the backrest possible.

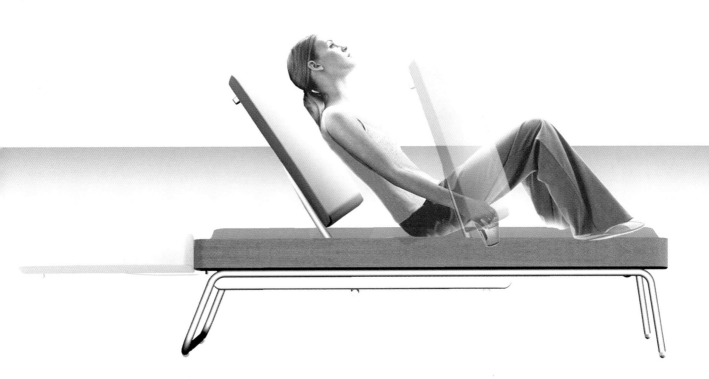

Moods bed/chaise/chair

The back rest slides, tilts, and lies flat.

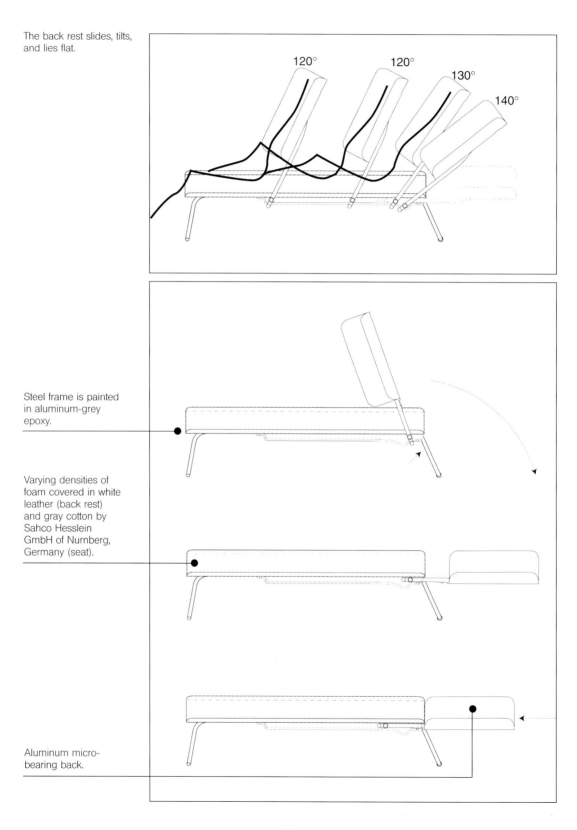

Steel frame is painted in aluminum-grey epoxy.

Varying densities of foam covered in white leather (back rest) and gray cotton by Sahco Hesslein GmbH of Nurnberg, Germany (seat).

Aluminum micro-bearing back.

Color palette of the upholstery materials.

The designer's developmental drawings.

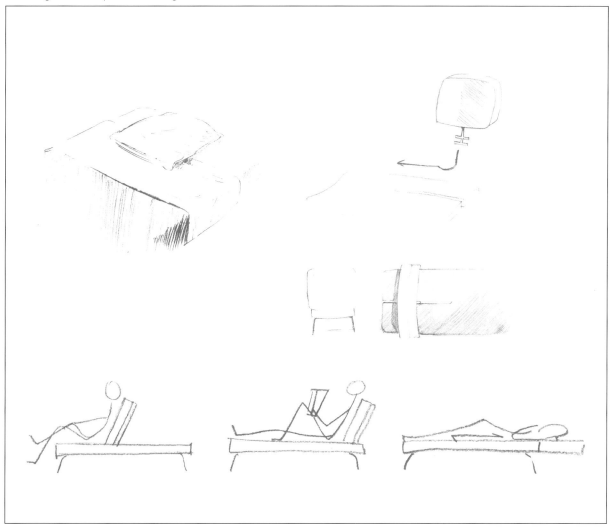

16

Llengua Meritxell

Designer: Jordi Torres Soca (Spanish)
Manufacturer: Torres & Torres,
Barcelona, Spain
Date of design: 1999

Even though traditional cabinet work and
upholstery techniques are used to produce this chaise-bed, the use of a shoe
(or shoe-sole) metaphor is striking, if not
bizarre.

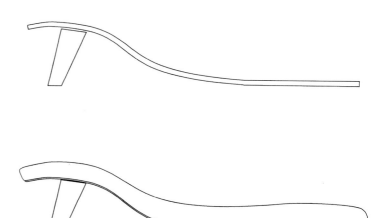

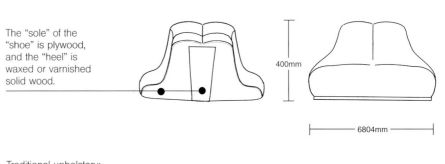

The "sole" of the
"shoe" is plywood,
and the "heel" is
waxed or varnished
solid wood.

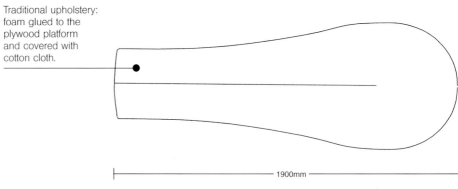

400mm

6804mm

Traditional upholstery:
foam glued to the
plywood platform
and covered with
cotton cloth.

1900mm

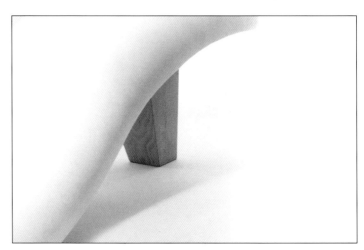

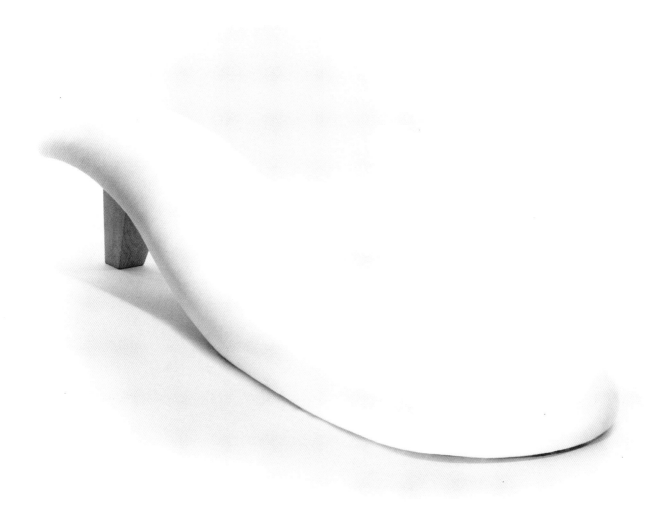

17

Chaise longue

Designer: Christian Ghion (French)
Manufacturer: IN.PRO.MAT for
Everstyle, France
Date of design: 2000

Calling on the use of a new material, this
chaise is not only unusual in its use of a gel
but also in its rakish cantilevered extensions
from a center pedestal. Whether the 24 donut-
shaped gel-filled lozenges in this prototype
offer comfort is not known.

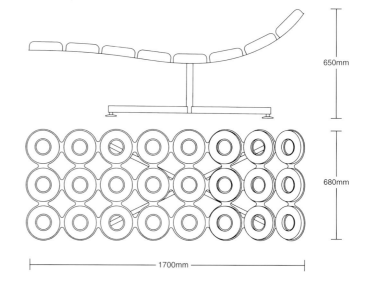

650mm

680mm

1700mm

24 highly resilient
molded polyurethane
viscoelastic gel
packs are glued to
the superstructure.

Laser-cut, bent, and
welded brushed alu-
minum superstructure.

18

Onda (Wave) chaise longue

Designer: Gianni Osgnach (Italian)
Manufacturer: Dilmos, Milano, Italy
Date of design: 1997

Since the creator of this piece is an artist and not a designer, the Onda is more a piece of art than a design object. The chaise is hand-painted to closely resemble the looks of a real wave after the longitudinal surface has been shaped with an electric cutter. The Onda is, of course, questionably comfortable.

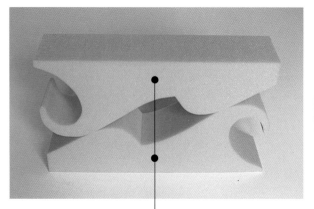

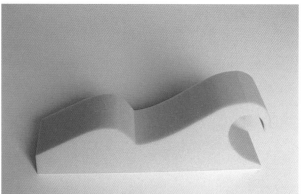

Two prototypes (above) are carved out, like the final version, with an electric cutter from a single block of polyurethane foam.

A maquette (right) has been painted to resemble the final chaise.

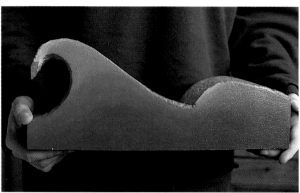

Final hand-finishing (bottom left and bottom right) illustrates more-detailed cutting and painting with colored resins.

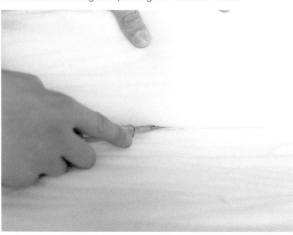

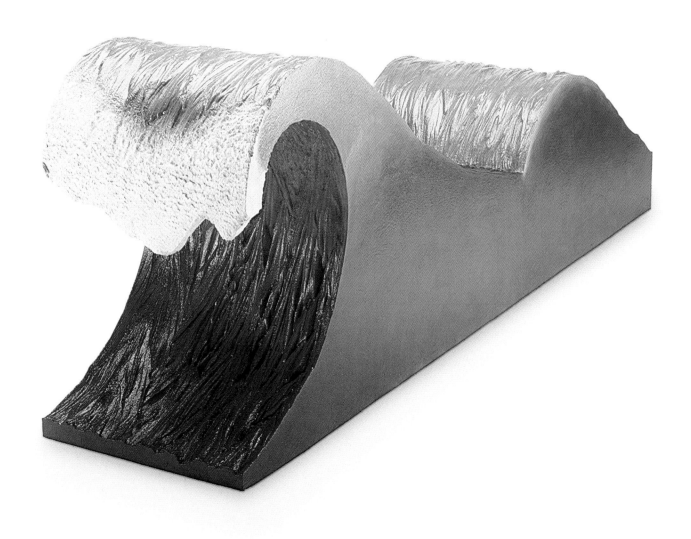

19

Mare Capovolto (Upside-Down Sea)

Designer: Francesco Filippi (Italian)
Manufacturer: Kreo, Milano (MI), Italy
Date of design: 1991

Admittedly this is an unusual bed, sofa, or whatever seat you wish to call it. Operated by an electric motor, this "upside-down sea" or "capsized ocean" is in the form of a softly shaped wave that produces the effect of two light waves. It features a tubular frame onto which a mechanism for producing two oscillatory movements is mounted. The wave effects in the three available models vary. The fourth model offers no movement at all.

Shown from below, the dimensions of the main versions of the seating device are 700 x 350mm high (with the back up).

Back support is the outer part of padding that is rolled up and kept in place by specially designed straps. It can also be laid straight (see below right).

A double layer of polyurethane rubber padding, back support, and fabric lining are attached to the tubular frame.

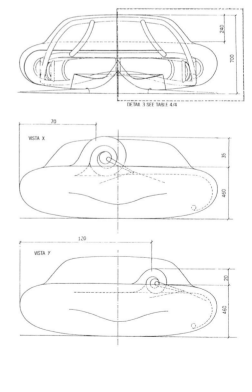

An asynchronous, single-phase motor (220v, 75kw) produces two movements: a wave effect along the vertical axis and two subtle waves running along the surface. The tubular frame is held by criss-cross layers of elastic nylon straps.

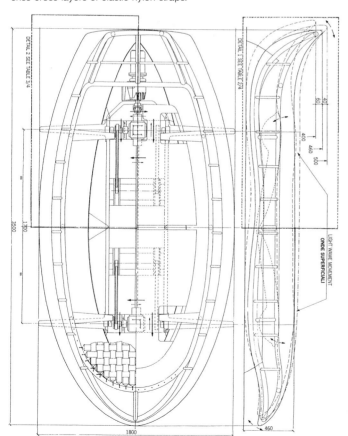

V.I.P.

Designer: Edward Zabuga (Russian)
Manufacturer: OOO Zabuga Furniture RPK,
Moscow, Russia
Date of design: 1996

Probably more a chaise longue than a bed,
the structure here is constructed from traditional materials. It features a cork-covered
headrest that, when lowered, becomes flush
with the top surface, also cork covered. The
numerous possibilities of other shapes is
illustrated by the version on page 68.

700mm

1700mm

800mm

800mm

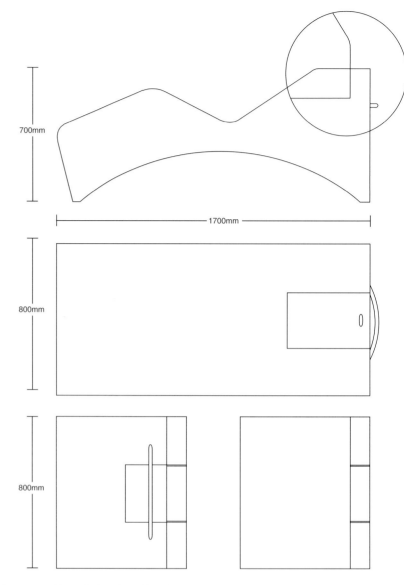

Cork-laminated
top surfaces.

The headrest is shown
in the raised position.

Frame in band- and hand-sawn plywood,
assembled with aluminum screws.

V.I.P.

Another interpretation of the chaise/table by the same designer, in a varnished,
laminated sandwich of plywood. The underside of the unit is hollow.

On the Floor

Sol mutable (Changeable Ground)

Designers: Thierry Gaugain, Patrick Jouin, and
Jean-Marie Massaud (all French)
Manufacturer: Luxlab, Paris, France (prototype)
Date of design: 1999

Contrary to the popular definition of "luxury" for which
the French have become known, this living surface is
an attempt by the designers to surpass what they
consider to be the controversial implications of the
word "luxury." Through various projects, like this live
indoor grass surface, they are exploring how the
poetry of an object might aspire to loftier ideals. Also,
they are asking, "What are the forms luxury requires
or can do without, and might the refined resultant still
be a luxury?" The Sol mutable system, which pursues
this refined idea of luxury, is intended symbolically and
materially to serve three sensuous experiences: lying
on grass, looking at water, and contemplating fire.

The "liquid-mirror" table
(1300 x 1300 x 380mm)
is composed of a mirror
and water, agitated by a
pump hidden in a leg of
the table. The lighting
system creates a moving
projection of light and
shadow. (See facing
page.)

Stainless-steel fireplace
(adjustable 600mm
height) with a Pyrex glass
duct and vacuum filter
eliminates the necessity
for a chimney.

Pressed
aluminum
frame.

Real, growing turf (or grass)
is automatically nourished
with microcapsules and
treated with a fungicide.

The surface is deformable
by air jacks and airbags
within the frame.

Dimensions: 2300 x 1500mm.

Snail bed/chaise

Designer: Fiona Davidson (British)
Manufacturer: the designer
Date of design: 1999

Seeking a conceptual solution to
domestic furniture, the rollable bed/
chaise is supplemented by a bolster.
Covered in fabric or leather, the
pallet can be coiled or uncoiled into
numerous configurations.

An uncovered prototype.

In a shape for sitting, the bed/chaise
illustrates its high malleability.

Reflex foam is cut
into shape with CNC
(computer-numeric-
control) sawing machinery.

When completely coiled, the form measures
700mm long x 600mm wide x 500mm deep.

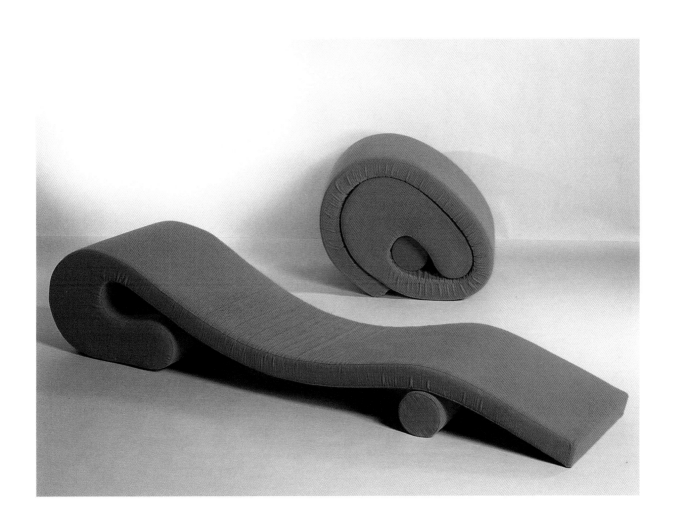

Magazine-Rug

Designer: Gitta Gschwendtner
(German)
Manufacturer: the designer
Date of design: 1998

The designer confesses to juxtaposing the expected with the unexpected by calling on surprise and humor. The object here, which questions conventional furniture standards and is used for reclining, combines bed, rug, and magazine-rack functions. The undulations in the rug appear to be quite casual, random and soft, but the formation of the fiberglass is quite intentional and far from casual, as the precise specifications in the designer's drawing (top right) indicates.

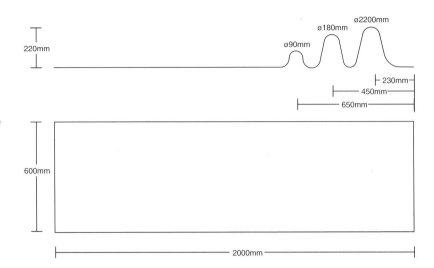

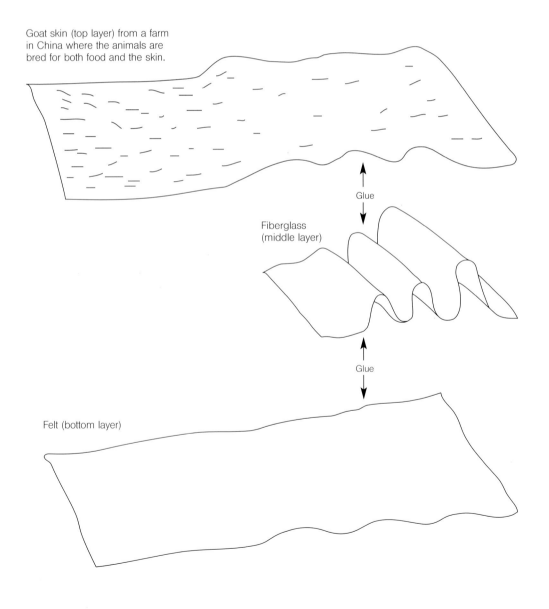

Goat skin (top layer) from a farm in China where the animals are bred for both food and the skin.

Glue

Fiberglass (middle layer)

Glue

Felt (bottom layer)

Pisoló (Nap), Pistolini (Short Nap), and Pisola

Designer: Denis Santachiara (Italian)
Manufacturer: Campeggi S.r.l., Anzano del Parco, Italy
Date of design: 1997

Described by the manufacturer as "an object that is both big and small and doesn't have to be stored away," the cheerful Pisoló version (right and below) of this bed series is kept in a hassock/table container when not in use. The elements include an electric air pump, the multi-functional hassock/table, and the inflatable bed itself. The synthetic materials used in the construction offer softness and discourage sweating. The Pistolini version of the bed (facing page) is housed in an orange, yellow, or gray transparent blue-polyester hassock with a PVC (polyvinyl-chloride) mattress. The Pisola version is a chair, rather than a hassock, that contains an inflatable mattress. (See page 79.)

Electric air pump.

The Pisoló version: lid (below left) and rolled-up bed housed in the bottom of the hassock (below right).

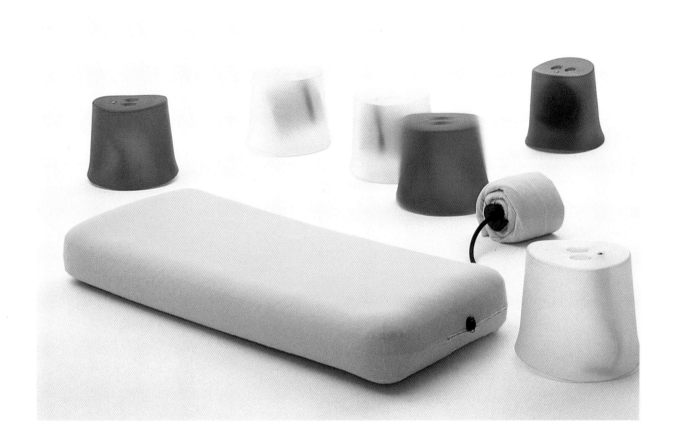

Pisoló (Nap), Pistolini (Short Nap), and Pisola

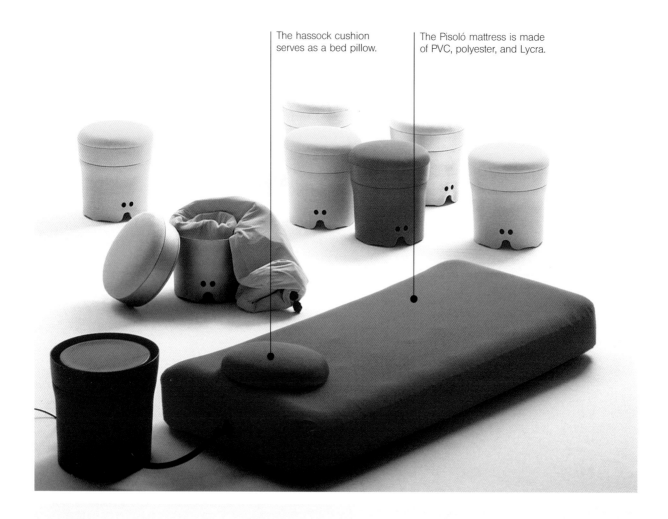

The hassock cushion serves as a bed pillow.

The Pisoló mattress is made of PVC, polyester, and Lycra.

The Pisola version is an armchair that contains the inflatable mattress and air pump.

Téo de 2 à 3

Designer: Matali Crasset (French)
Manufacturer: Domeau & Pérès, La Garenne
Colombes, France
Date of design: 1999

The designer of this sleeping unit has worked
with Denis Santachiara (see page 76–79) and
at Thomson Multimedia under Philippe Starck.
The Téo de 2 à 3 is produced by a saddler
and an upholsterer in a firm which was estab-
lished in 1996–97. The hassock element of the
unit contains a bed designed to be used for a
siesta during the lunch break at a workplace.

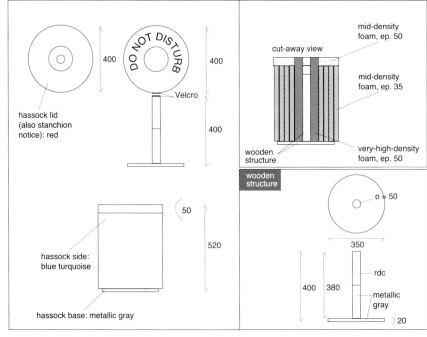

hassock lid
(also stanchion
notice): red

Velcro

400

400

400

DO NOT DISTURB

hassock side:
blue turquoise

50

520

hassock base: metallic gray

cut-away view

mid-density
foam, ep. 50

mid-density
foam, ep. 35

wooden
structure

very-high-density
foam, ep. 50

wooden
structure

o = 50

350

rdc

metallic
gray

400   380

20

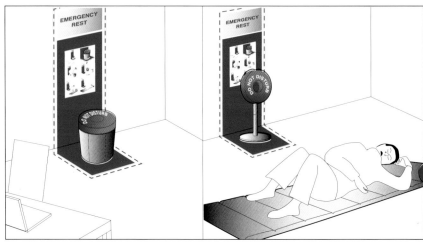

EMERGENCY
REST

EMERGENCY
REST

Xito

Designer: Giovanni Levanti (Italian)
Manufacturer: Campeggi S.r.l.,
Anzano del Parco, Italy
Date of design: 1997

This multifunctional, multipurpose seat for reading, watching television, operating a portable computer, sleeping, relaxing, exercising, or playing can be arranged at different angles. It is defined by what it is not; it is not a sofa, chair, or mattress.

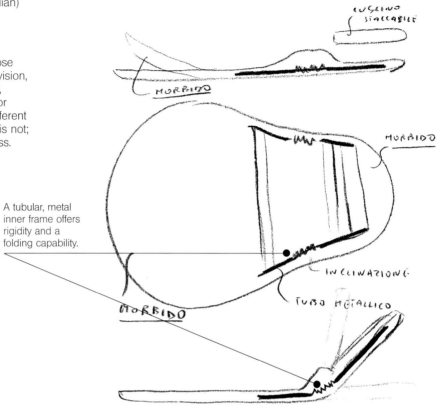

A tubular, metal inner frame offers rigidity and a folding capability.

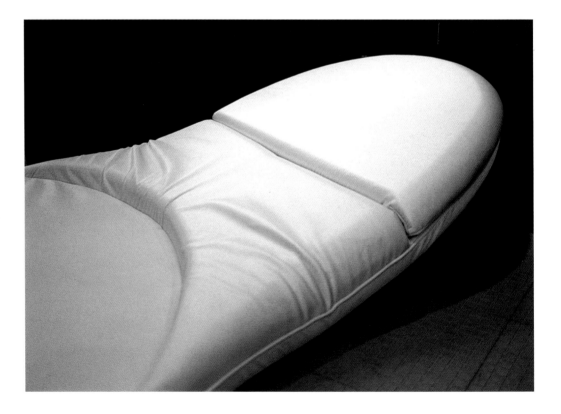

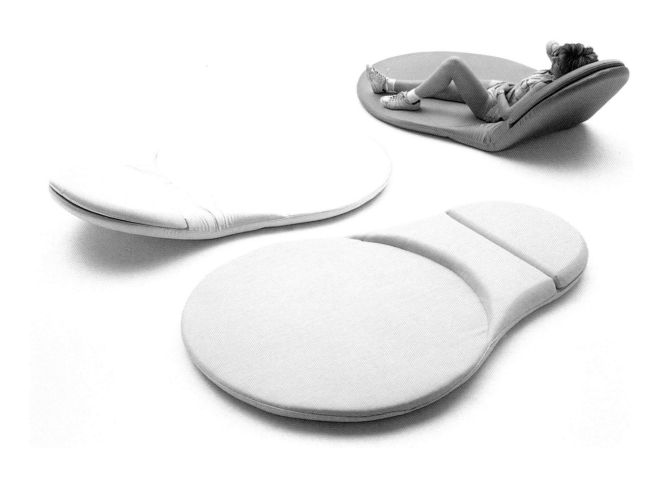

Xito

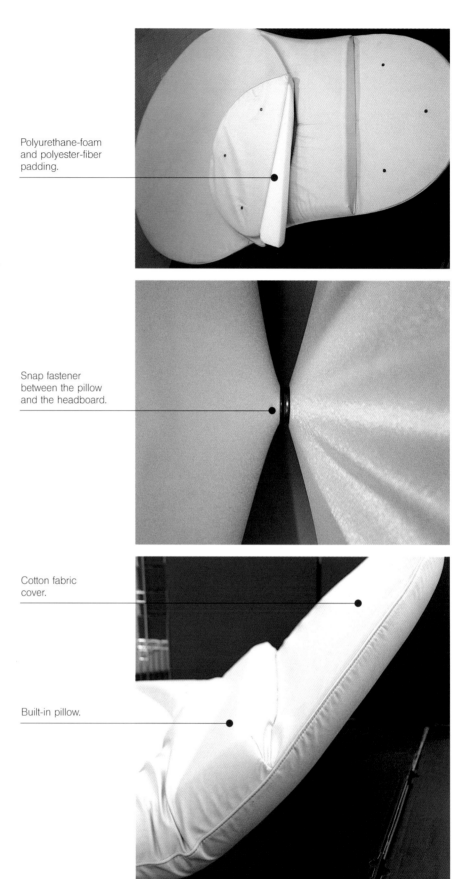

Polyurethane-foam
and polyester-fiber
padding.

Snap fastener
between the pillow
and the headboard.

Cotton fabric
cover.

Built-in pillow.

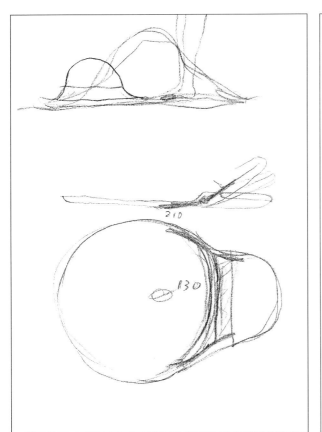

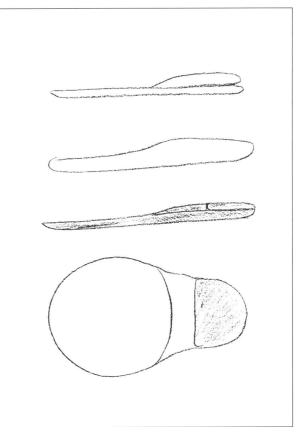

Some designer developmental drawings.

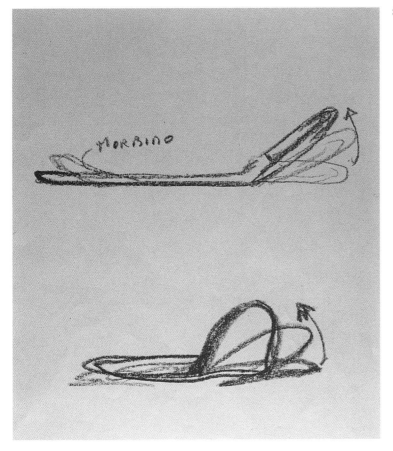

27

Peace

Designer: Alfredo Häberli (Swiss-Argentine)
Manufacturer: the designer
Date of design: 1991

A rectangular piece of felt is folded into a three-dimensional shape to form a bed/chaise/carpet unit. Except for copper buttons and the felt fabric, no other materials are used. Currently felt is a fashionable material not only for clothing but also in home furnishings.

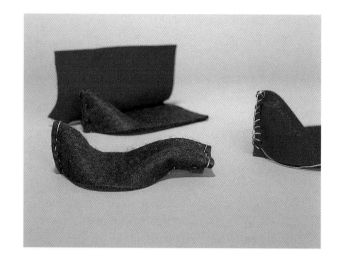

Felt rectangular: 1000 x 2000 x 40mm thick.

One of the six copper buttons.

Experimental maquettes (above and top).

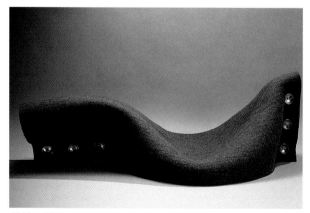

1000 x 2000mm felt rectangle, when flat.

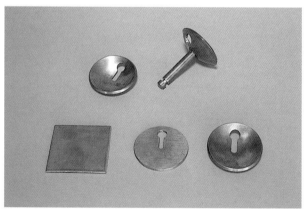

Copper buttons (stays and flanges).

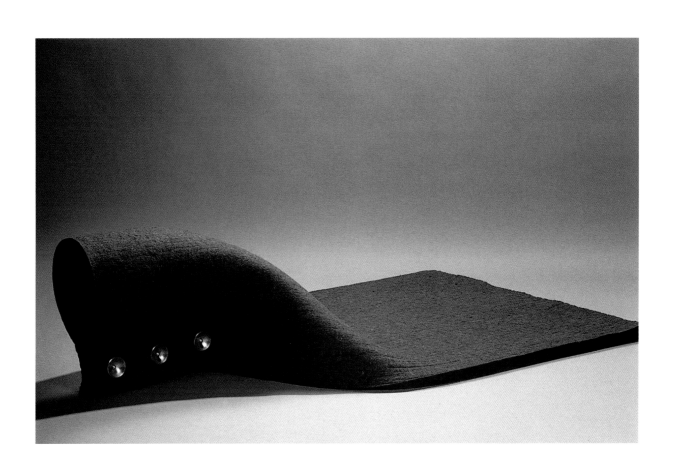

28

Espace TV

Designer: Nestor Perkal (French)
Manufacturer: Chez Valentin, Paris, France
Date of design: 1999

The prototype bed/lounge/television/
cabinet combination here is the
designer's interpretation of the essential
furnishings and equipment of today's
living. Perkal has amalgamated the
elements found in the average
bedroom into a single unit, which he
calls the "TV area."

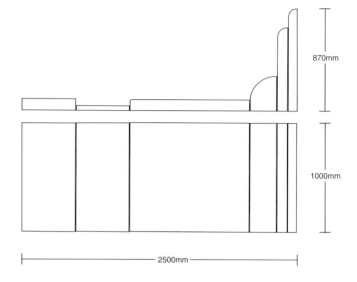

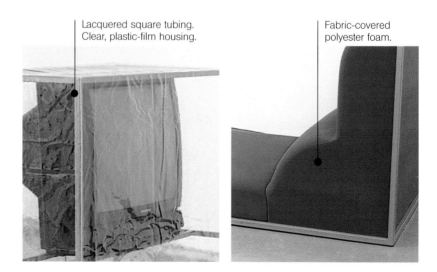

The designer's preliminary study.

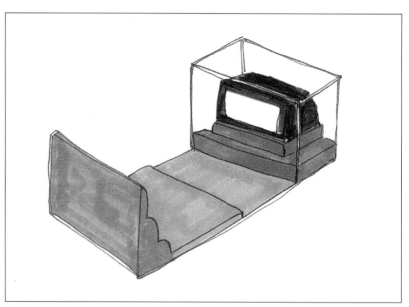

Lacquered square tubing.
Clear, plastic-film housing.

Fabric-covered
polyester foam.

29

Nomad Carpet

Designer: Marcel Wanders (Dutch)
Manufacturer: Cappellini S.p.A., Arosio
(CO), Italy
Date of design: 1998

According to the designer, this bed/carpet
serves what he claims is a basic need for
simple furniture with flexible functionality. He
further suggests that "there is a basic need
to be closer to the floor, to be grounded
and relaxed and closer to the warm belly of
Mother Earth." The construction materials
of the Nomad Carpet include thick high-
quality wool carpeting and high-grade
plywood. The angle of the backrest is
positionable at one of three angles.

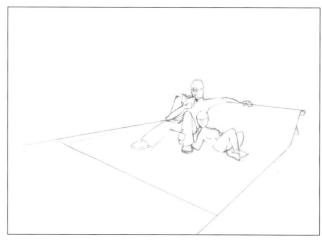

Laser-cut
waterproof
plywood.

Hidden mecha-
nism permits
three angles of
incline.

Beige, brown, or gray
long-hair wool carpet,
treated with a natural
latex that fixes the wool
and thwarts slippage.

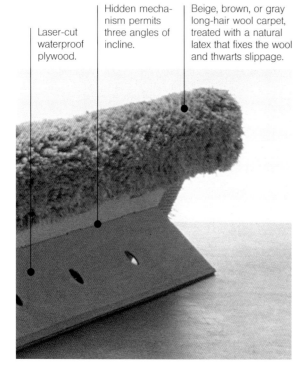

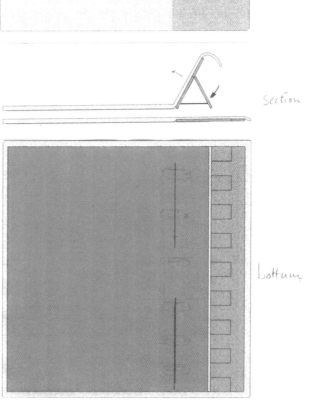

30

Lotus daybed

Designer: Pierre Bouguennec (French)
Manufacturer: Boum Design, New York,
NY, U.S.A.
Date of design: 1999

In the world of today's easily accessible
high-tech materials, the surface for this
daybed is more labor-intensive than one
might suspect. Each suction cup is
hand-attached to individually bored
holes in the two-material sandwich.

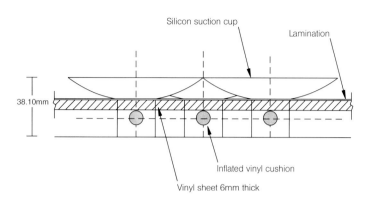

Silicon suction cup

Lamination

38.10mm

Inflated vinyl cushion

Vinyl sheet 6mm thick

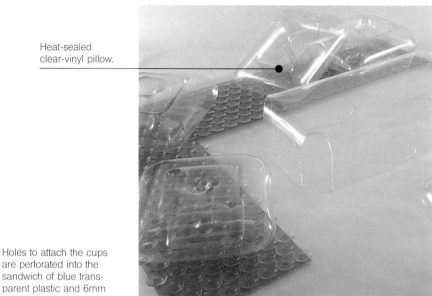

Heat-sealed
clear-vinyl pillow.

Each silicon
suction cup is
manually
attached.

Holes to attach the cups
are perforated into the
sandwich of blue trans-
parent plastic and 6mm
vinyl sheeting.

31

Red Bed and Black Bed

Designer: Matt Sindall (British)
Manufacturer: Tramico, Paris, France
Date of design: 1996

The designer's inspiration for this bed began with a
visit to the Tramico factory. He discovered that the
facility uses an Albrech-Baumer high-frequency
O.F.S. saw capable of cutting mono-block foam in
profiles as wide as 2.5m. The one-piece bed here
holds the user's body aloft on foam fingers, integrated extensions of the one-piece construction.
The profile is numerically determined, and then the
foam is cut horizontally and vertically. A complex,
rather than typically flat, form was created in order
to communicate an image not normally associated
with foam, particularly foam mattresses.

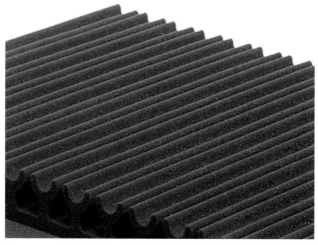

The repeated "Y"-shape pattern in polyether foam suspends the
sleeper's body.

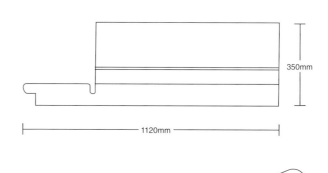

350mm

1120mm

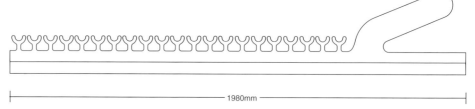

1980mm

The one-piece form in polyether
foam incorporates a headrest
that replaces a pillow.

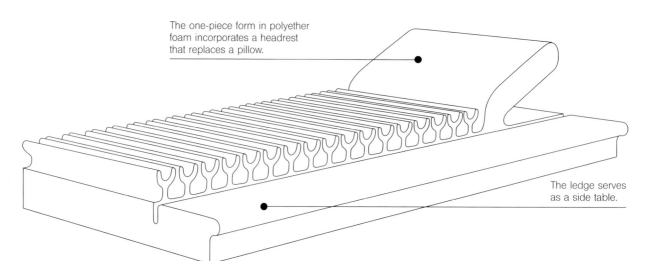

The ledge serves
as a side table.

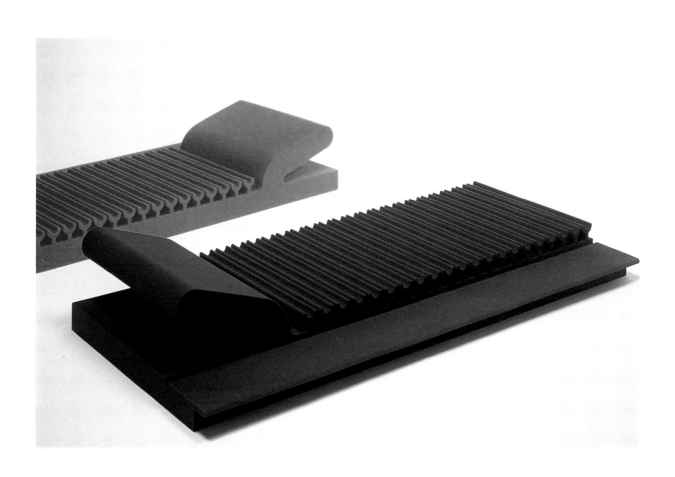

32

IKEA a.i.r./poppig

Designer: Jan Dranger (Swedish)
Manufacturer: News Design DFE A.B., Stockholm,
Sweden, for IKEA
Date of design: 1997

Possibly a little precious, "a.i.r." is an acronym for "air
is a resource." The SoftAir™ manufacturer claims that
furniture made with its new technology—including
sofas, chairs, and this bed—uses less energy during
its life cycle than traditional furniture. Purportedly the
raw materials required to make a SoftAir™ sofa are
approximately 15% of that of a traditional sofa of the
same size and it occupies only about 10% of its
space during warehousing and transportation. The air
compartments are made of a so-called olefin plastic,
the purest plastic available and 100% recyclable. The
lid and the "air-control" stick are made of polypropy-
lene which is also fully recyclable.

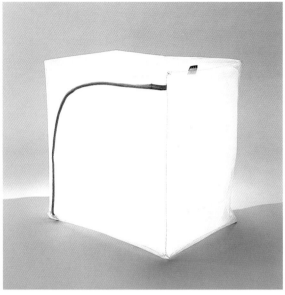

A zipper sack (above) holds a deflated bed. A duvet-type
sleeve covers the seven compartments of a fully inflated
mattress (facing page).

The furniture is manufactured with equipment by the German
firm Mauser. The air compartments do not have welded seams
but are manufactured in one single piece with an airtight sealing
cap that eliminates air leakage. Topping off the air is necessary
only at three-year intervals.

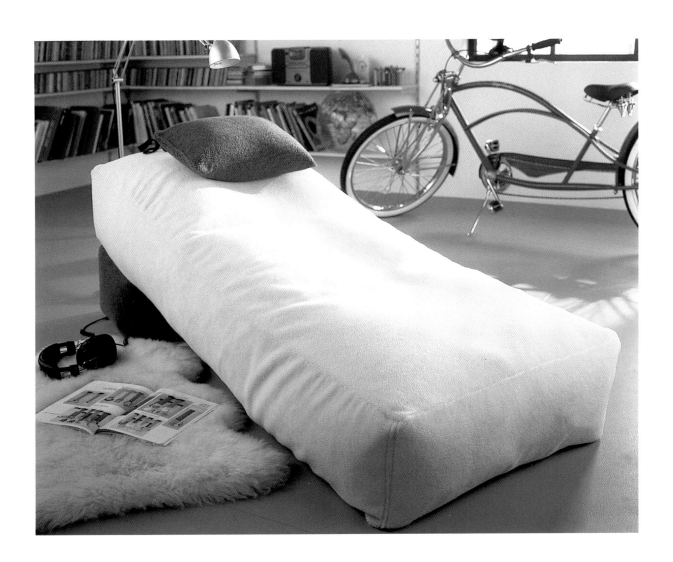

IKEA a.i.r./poppig

a.i.r./poppig is the first long-life, flat-packed upholstered furniture. SoftAir™ furniture—inflatable with a hair-dryer—is made up of a number of separate air-filled "cells," manufactured from fully recyclable, soft polyolefin. It is more comfortable to sit on than PVC (polyvinylchloride) and an environmental improvement over PVC.

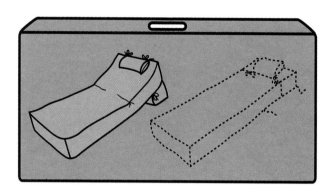

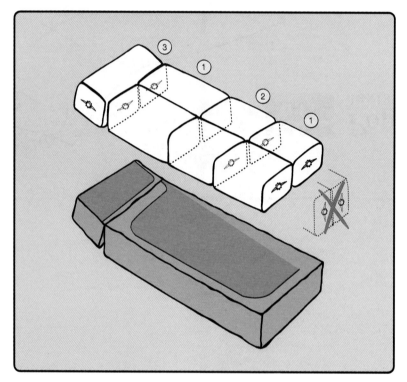

Convertibles

33

Ormeggio (Mooring)

Designer: Pepi Tanzi (Italian)
Manufacturer: Biesse S.p.A., Lissone (MI), Italy
Date of design: 1995

The sales literature for this daybed claims that it is suitable for "domestic tourism," in other words, for guests. Comfortable and large, the wide, jointed, metallic backrest-bow is an element of the efficient folding-away mechanism that permits the mattress to be fully unencumbered when the three-person sofa is converted to a one-person bed. (Another convertible bed produced by Biesse is featured on page 106.)

Two feather-stuffed pillows.

Natural-fiber stuffed mattress (1950 x 900 x 250mm); optional extra mattress and pillow covers available.

Wooden self-stopping wheels with rubber treads.

Fold-back bow, part of the tubular-steel frame and folding mechanism, coated with gray, violet, or bronze transparent, brilliant, and metallic epoxy paint.

Springy beechwood slats.

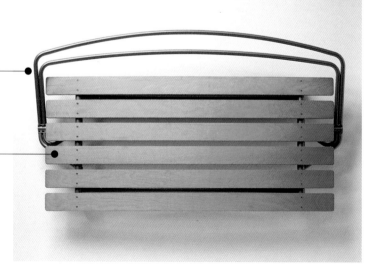

Lunar and Zzofá convertibles

Designer: James Irvine (British) .
Manufacturer: Lunar: B&B Italia S.p.A.,
Novedrate (CO), Italy; Zzofá: Cappellini S.p.A.,
Arosio (CO), Italy
Date of design: 1993 and 1998

The two similar beds here are by the same
designer, but they are produced by two
different firms and operate based on two
entirely different principles. The cover of the
Lunar, (shown on this and the facing page)
is removable. The drawings at the right
instruct the user on how to change the sofa
into a bed: stand in front of the sofa and pull
the seat forward by pulling on a metal bar
(A), while, at the same time, you hold the
small tube (B). Then you press the pedal
(C) down and, finally, lower the backrest.
And, of course, to re-form the bed, the
operation is reversed.

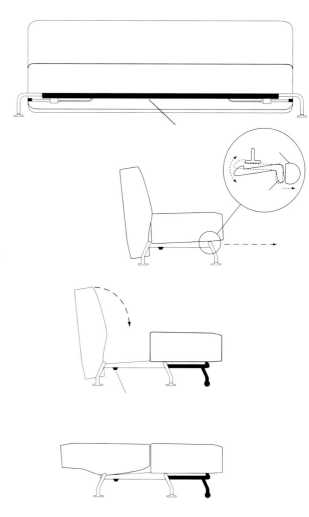

Back and seat are single-
padded polyurethane
blocks with fully removable
fabric covers for cleaning.

Gray metallic varnished
tubular-steel frame.

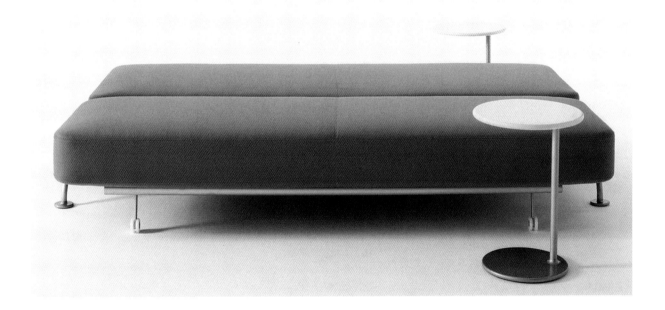

34

Zzofá and Lunar

On the Zzofá bed, another convertible by the same designer but by a different firm, the gasplunger mechanisms permit the rotation of the backrest.

Metal parts are painted in anti-crack aluminum-color lacquer.

The metal frame is covered with polyurethane foam. Upholstery is either removable fabric or unremovable leather.

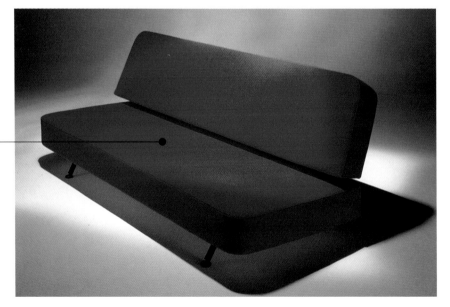

35

Aliante (Glider)

Designer: Bruno Saibene, Biesse staff
Manufacturer: Biesse S.p.A., Lissone
(MI), Italy
Date of design: 1995

The name of this convertible refers to its purported ease of operation—effortlessly gliding from sofa to double bed. The tubular-steel frame is painted to look like aluminum. The perforations in the wooden platform offer flexibility and aerate the mattress. The rear wheels permit mobility, and the shiny fabric adds glamour. (Another convertible bed produced by Biesse is featured on page 100.)

Aluminum-epoxy-paint-coated tubular-steel structure.

Flexible beechwood is perforated for ventilation and flex.

Rear wheels offer ease of operation.

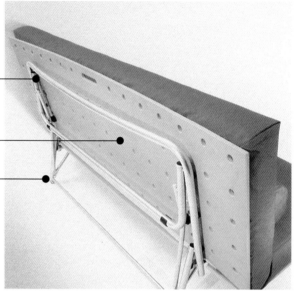

Expanded-polyurethane double-size orthopedic bed (1950 x 1400 x 870mm high) is covered in an iridescent fabric. The bolsters are multifunctional.

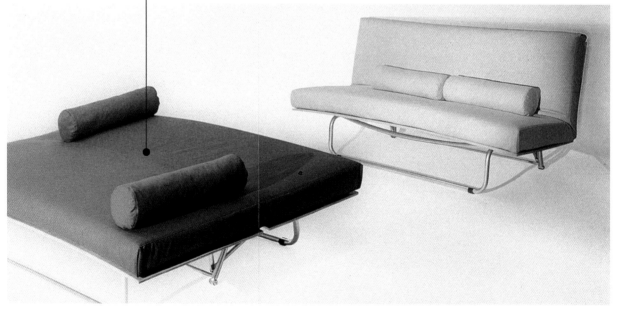

36

St. Michel

Designer: Marc Sadler (French)
Manufacturer: Orizzonti S.r.l., Misinto (MI), Italy
Date of design: 1996

A guest bed appears to have been transformed by magic from what looks like only an ordinary hassock. The structure extends like an accordion from the wire cage that holds the mattress, which is covered by a duvet, and likewise unfolds from three sections.

Wheels assist the frame's extension from the mattress cage.

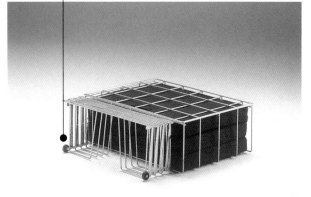

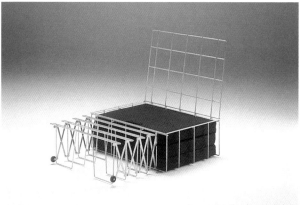

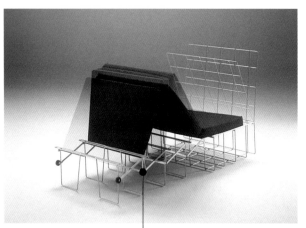

Folding structure (in action here) in chromium-plated steel rods.

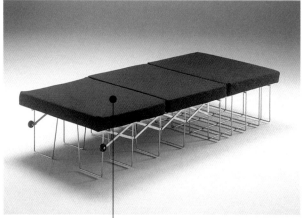

A two-fold mattress (1950 x 850mm) and a half-size duvet filled with 100% duck feathers is covered in 100g/sqm non-allergic muslin. Since standard sheets are difficult to fit onto guest beds, zipper fasteners on each side and buttons for attaching white sheets with buttonholes make this set-up easier.

37

Tira & Molla (Stretchy & Soft)

Designer: Roberto Lucci and Paolo Orlandini
(both Italian)
Manufacturer: Biesse S.p.A., Lissone (MI), Italy
Date of design: 1993

This piece of furniture is available in one, two, or
three widths. Suitable for small living spaces, the
folding device permits its use as a bed, chaise
longue, or sofa. The mattress features a 120mm
differentiated thickness. The designers who
collaborated on this bed have also been known
to work alone.

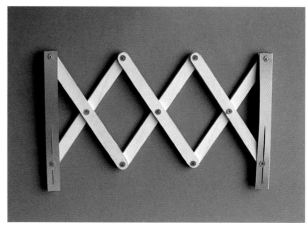

A designer's study maquette of the folding mechanism.

The folding mechanism permits easy extension from a sofa position (below) to that of chaise longue (right) to a bed (facing page).

The upholstery cover acts like an envelope or hood over foam
rubber. The feet have build-in wheels.

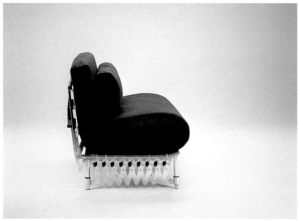

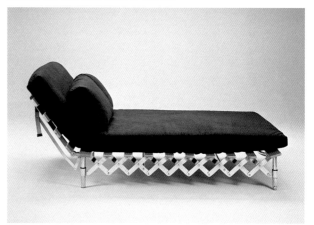

Beech plywood
slats.

Riveted die-cast aluminum
and gray epoxy-painted or
chromium-plated tubular steel.

Compare the Lucci/Orlandini bed with the folding camp-bed that
Peter Stuyvesant gave to George Washington in 1780.

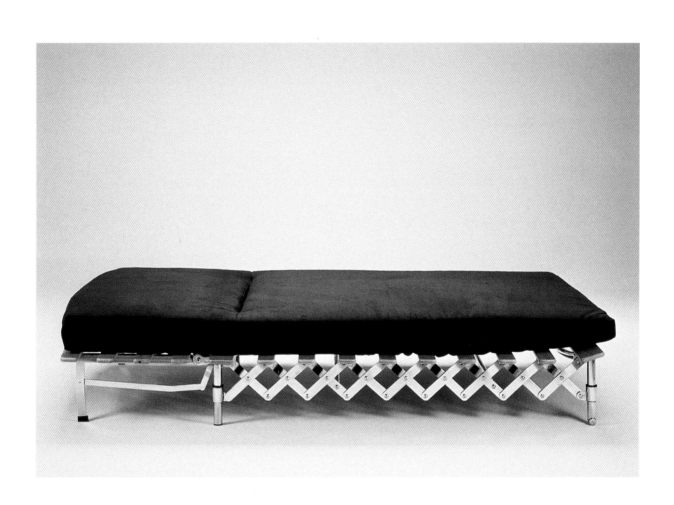

38

Ospite (Guest) daybed

Designer: Vico Magistretti (Italian)
Manufacturer: Campeggi S.r.l., Anzano del
Parco (CO), Italy
Date of design: 1996

When opened, the Ospite becomes a daybed
or, with the addition of the back dowel, a sofa.
As a sofa, of course, a number of pillows
rather than the single example shown here
would be necessary; however, comfort does
not appear to be the primary feature. This
piece of furniture is possibly more interesting
as a feat of engineering than as a fully
functional bed.

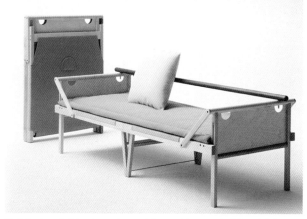

Polished, unfinished maplewood frame. Linen upholstery fabric.
Shown open (above right) and folded flat (above left).

1

2

Four stages of the unfolding of the flat bed are illustrated here.
When it is folded flat (above), the size is a mere 130 x 1090mm
and the mattress (not shown) is rolled up.

3

4

39

Sydney

Designer: Stefan Heiliger (Swiss)
Manufacturer: Interprofil AG, Lüterkofen,
Switzerland
Date of design: 1993

As a sofa, the Sydney reveals no clues that
it can be transformed into a bed as comfortable as any high-quality mattress. It can be
converted into either a daybed with the back
erect or, when the back is folded down, a
double bed.

Dimensions: 2140 x 890 x 710mm high, as a sofa.

The aluminum armature
that permits the sofa-bed
conversions.

Two bed stages—a daybed
(right) and a double bed (facing
page)—are made possible by the
aluminum armature that slides
back along the slit between the
mattress and the base.

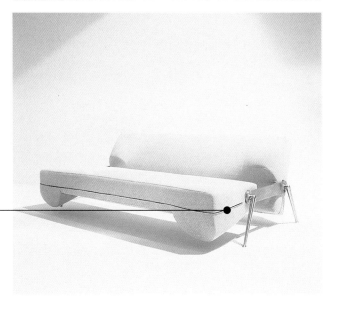

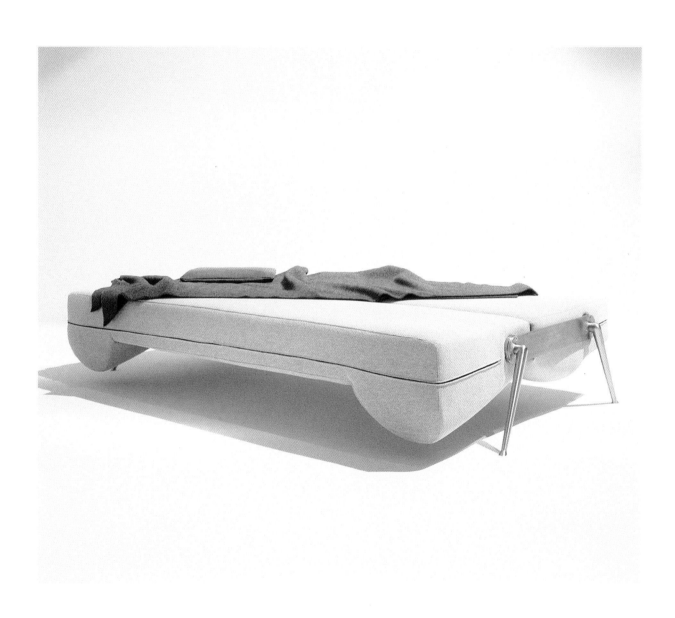

Cabrio™ 80 and 120 desk/bed

Designer: Giulio Manzoni (Italian)
Manufacturer: Clei S.r.l., Carugo (CO), Italy
Date of design: 1998

One in a group of ingenious convertible bedding units by Clei, the configuration here is available in either a single- or double-bed size. It is appropriate as the sole bed in a small dwelling or as one to accommodate guests. Unlike the convertible here, the structural elements of the Doc™, by the same designer and manufacturer, are hidden. (See pages 118–20.)

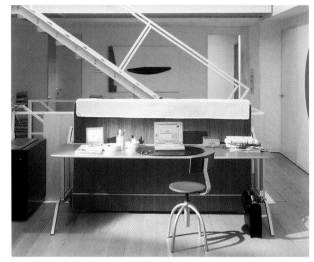

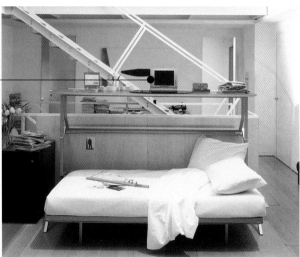

Items on the desktop may remain in place when the bed is open.

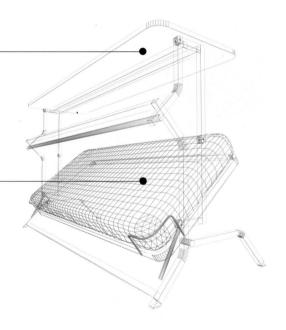

Desk top (2100 x 600mm).

The height of the unit is 1730mm when the bed is down and 800mm or 1200mm high (depending on single- or double-mattress sizes) when the bed is folded back and the desk is down.

Doc™ sofa/bunk bed

Designer: Giulio Manzoni (Italian)
Manufacturer: Clei S.r.l., Carugo (CO), Italy
Date of design: 1998

In addition to the Cabrio desk/bed on the preced-
ing pages and other models in the Clei range, the
Giulio Manzoni's solutions to multi-use bedding is
aesthetically pleasing, technologically innovative,
and downright ingenious. Should you not be
aware of its secret, you would never know that the
sofa at the right can easily and quickly be transformed into bunk beds.

As the drawing illustrates, the
top mattress folds down and
under the sofa seat cushion
and its back edge faces out.

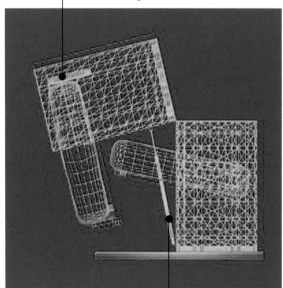

The piston mechanism
permits the unit to be
converted effortlessly
from bunk beds to sofa
or vice versa.

1290mm high (bed opened);
950 to top of sofa (bed folded up).

Sheets and blankets do not need
removing when the conversion
occurs, thus offering a ready-to-
use bed at any time.

Doc™ sofa/bunk beds

Like an insect from its chrysalid state, the sofa unfolds from a sofa into bunk beds.

Cribs and Children's Beds

42

Cerise bed

Designer: Vincent Becheau and Marie-Laure Bourgeois
(both French)
Manufacturer: the designers
Date of design: 1995

Turned-wood columns have been combined with
panels to produce a bed intended for children. Fitted
together like a wooden toy, the bed evokes compar-
isons to ancient Chinese, and possibly even Moorish,
examples. When fitted with a mattress, children will
probably find this unit fascinating and fun.

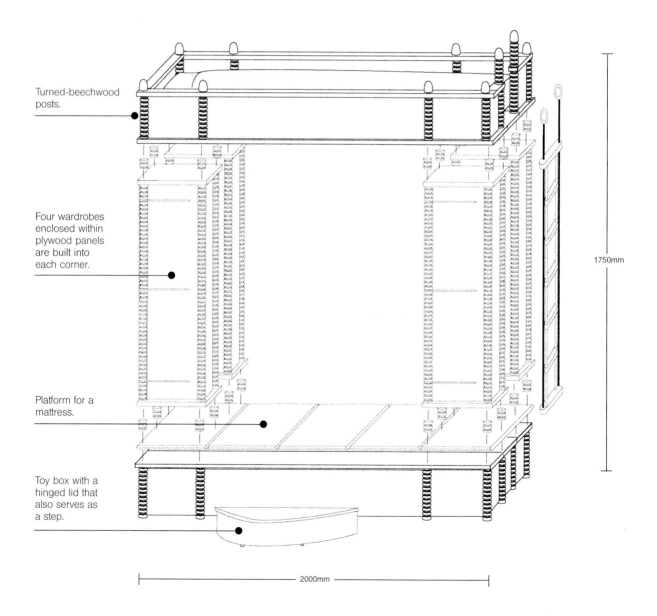

Turned-beechwood
posts.

Four wardrobes
enclosed within
plywood panels
are built into
each corner.

Platform for a
mattress.

Toy box with a
hinged lid that
also serves as
a step.

1750mm

2000mm

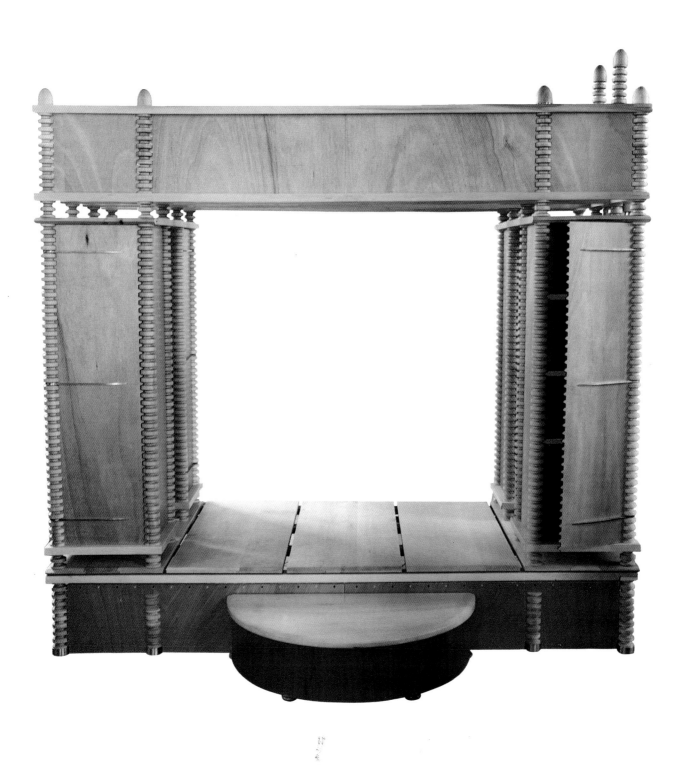

43

Cradle

Designer: Ole Gjerløv-Knudsen (Danish)
Manufacturer: Assidomän, Dansk Kraftemballage,
Kolding, Denmark
Date of design: 1996

This inexpensive cardboard cradle is intended as
an alternative to wooden cradles in traditional
materials. As parents know, a cradle occupies
much-needed space and becomes obsolete
when the child requires a standard bed. This version, the three parts of which are to be assembled
by the customer, is held together by the mattress
and the baby's weight. After use, it can be dis-
carded and recycled without regard for its value.

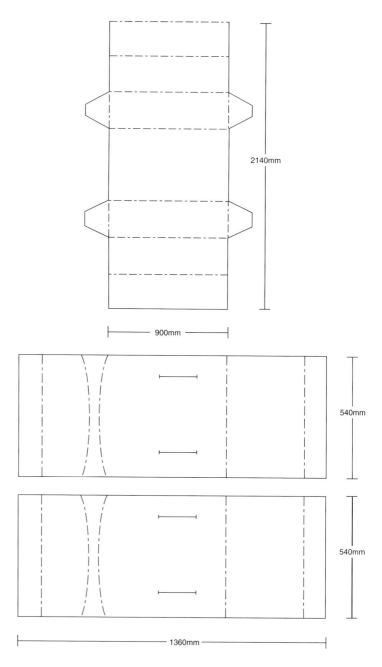

The customer purchases
this inexpensive cradle in
its flat-packed form, tied
with a cord.

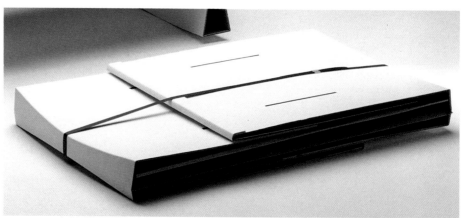

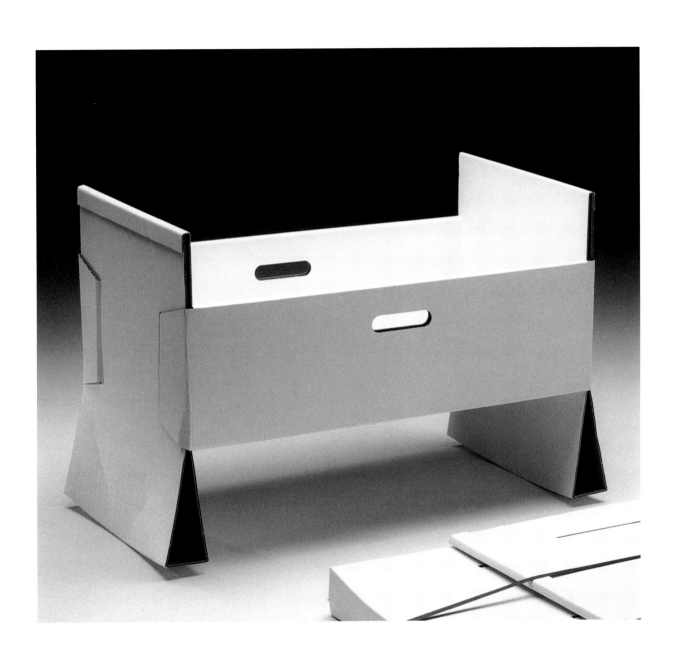

44

Swing Low

Designer: Sup Design—Søren Ulrik Petersen
(Danish)
Manufacturer: Sup Design, Korsgade,
Denmark
Date of design: 1997

This cradle is to be self-assembled by the
user. The materials in the kit consist of three
felt pieces, some hemp cord, a metal ceiling
hook, and a mattress with a zippered cover.
Instructions suggest that the cradle hang
from the hook provided, not hold more than
80kg, not be farther than one meter above
the parents' bed, be placed over a soft rug
should the cradle be hung over a hard floor,
not be placed near a fire, be locked in
a fixed position when the baby inside is
unsupervised, and be removed from com-
mission if any part is missing or torn.

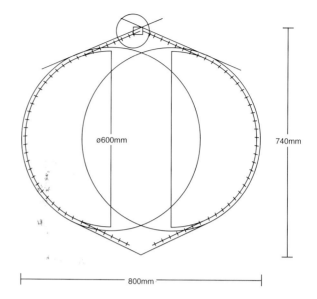

ø600mm   740mm   800mm

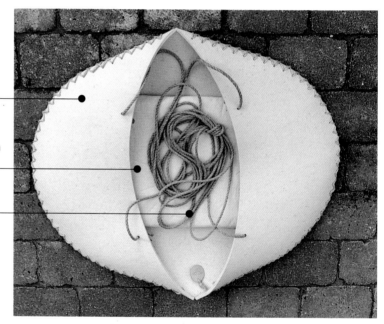

Wool-felt body.

Mattress in wool felt with
zippered washable cotton
cover.

Hemp cord.

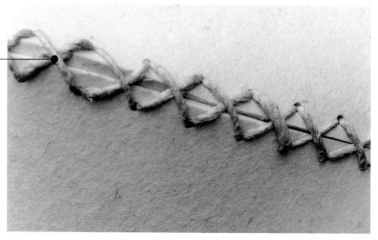

Self-assembled by tread-
ing hemp cord through
pre-perforated holes.

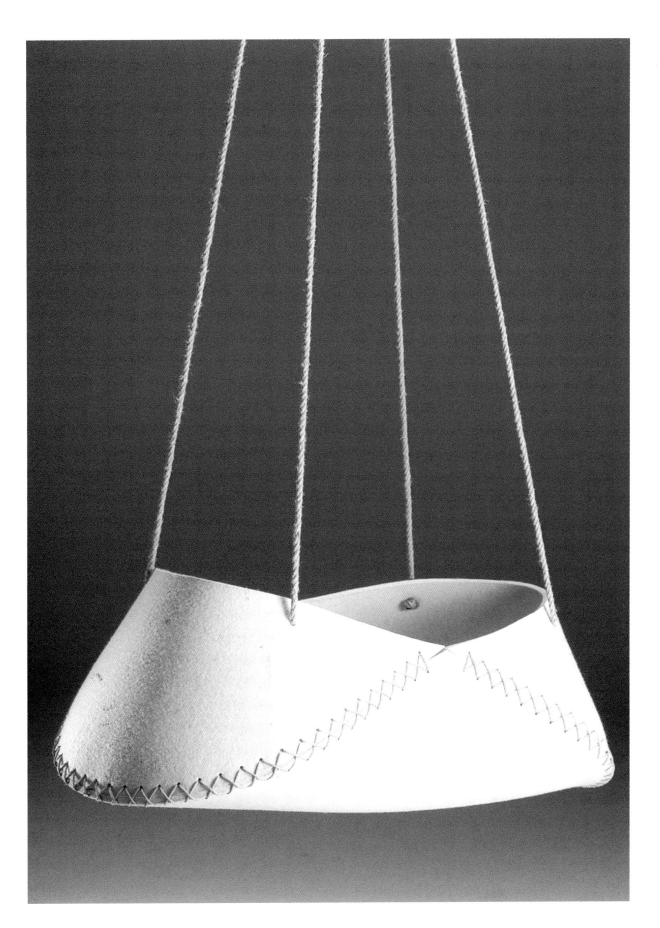

45

Ninna

Designer: Cecilia Amman (Italian)
Manufacturer: Plino Il Giovane, Milano, Italy
Date of design: 1995

According to the designer, this plywood bed is designed to be within easy reach of the parents' bed. Like an eggshell, it warmly surrounds the baby with no sharp angles. The cradle is produced by CNC pantography and finished with a resistant oil by Solas. It is assembled through slotting and with pegs, but no glue, screws, or potentially harmful materials are necessary for assembly. When knocked down, the unit can be stored and economically shipped.

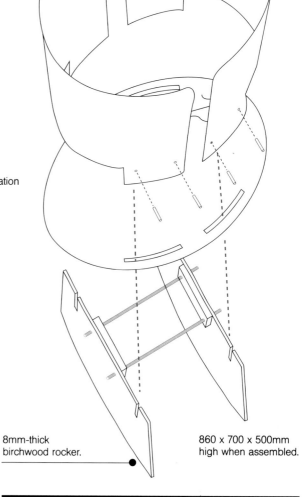

4mm-thick bent birchwood.

8mm-thick birchwood base.

20mm ventilation holes.

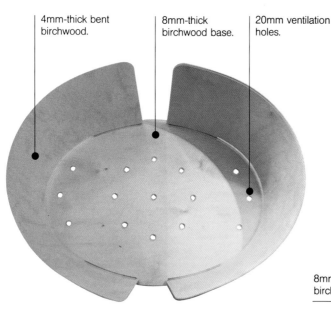

8mm-thick birchwood rocker.

860 x 700 x 500mm high when assembled.

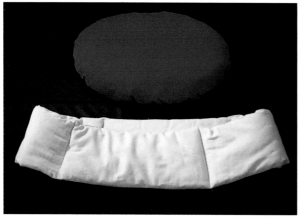

Mattress (red) and circular padded liner (white) in 100% cotton.

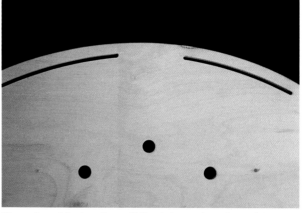

Close view of the base's ventilation holes and, on the periphery, the outer slots into which the sides are inserted, eliminating a need for fasteners or glue.

46

Marghe crib/cot

Designer: Francesco Pasquali Frederico
Giaume (Italian)
Manufacturer: Squadramobile, Milano (MI), Italy
Date of design: 1995

Light Scandinavian wood is used to produce
this crib or cot which is an assemblage of
fabric, buttons, slats, and belts. The mattress
can be positioned at three different heights
and altered to accommodate a child's growth
from three months to three years. Shipped
flat-packed, self-assembly is required.

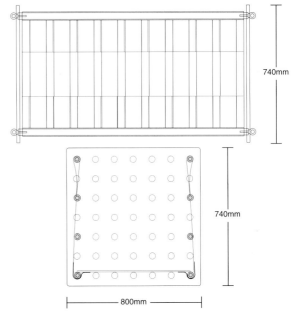

740mm

740mm

800mm

Mattress and side
dowels can be posi-
tioned differently, at
the same time.

35mm
holes.

18mm-thick multilay-
ered Finnish birch-
wood end panels.

Examples (below) of low
and high mattresses.

Stainless-steel
eye bolts.

Four longitudinal
ø35mm beech-
wood dowels,
with stainless-
steel eye bolts at
the ends, are
inserted through
the holes of the
end panels for
positioning the
mattress.

Beechwood bent
slats inserted into
the side fabric.

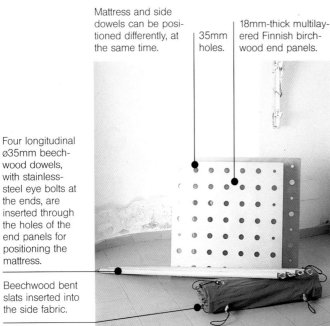

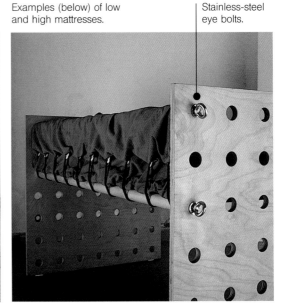

Buttons through
holes hold the
fabric side panels
taut at the top.

50% cotton/
50% flax fabric.

Elastic bands
around buttons
hold the fabric
side panels taut
at the bottom.

47

Barchetta (Dinghy)

Designer: Huub Ubbens (Dutch)
Manufacturer: Malofancon S.n.c., Malo (VI), Italy
Date of design: 1989

Even though this crib was designed in 1989, it was not put into production until 1995. The design permits the body of the crib to rock omnidirectionally. In a naturally finished light-colored wood, the object is essentially a small floating space for an infant.

A view from the top (below) shows the ventilation holes beneath the mattress.

Wool mattress with cotton batting (not shown).

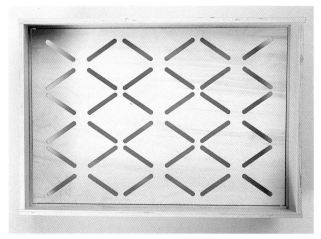

Russian birch plywood (from 15000 x 1500mm boards), finished with a hot bio-ecological oil/wax mixture applied with a spray gun.

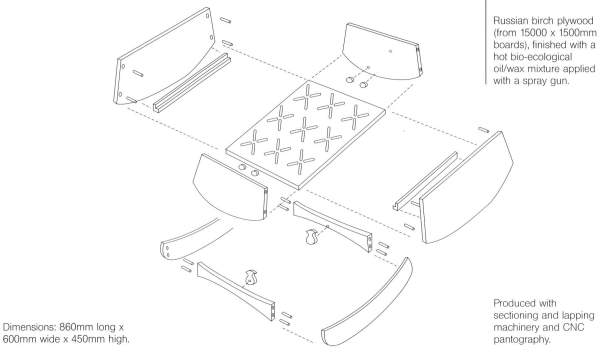

Dimensions: 860mm long x 600mm wide x 450mm high.

Produced with sectioning and lapping machinery and CNC pantography.

48

Sloophouten Ledikant (Scrap Wood)

Designer: Piet-Hein Eek (Dutch)
Manufacturer: Eek en Ruijgrok vof, Geldrop,
the Netherlands
Date of design: 1996

Were the date and geographical origin of this design
not provided here, it would be impossible to know its
time and place. Obviously built with a saw and scrap
lumber, the variety found in the configuration of most
cribs can, of course, be found here (see right and
facing page). Common concerns of manufacturers
and purchasers of cribs, including this example,
include low cost and short time of use. Since this
crib began as material that was refuse, low cost and
concern over limited use are negligible.

Cache of scrap lumber
that the designer/builder
calls on.

The construction of these cribs is obvious. The infant version is
shown below and on the facing page, and the small-child version
is at the lower right and top of this page.

Tamagó

Designer: Liévore Associates—Alberto Liévore
(Argentine), Jeannette Altherr (German), and
Manel Molina (Spanish)
Manufacturer: Orizzonti, Gruppo I.C.A. S.r.l.,
Misinto, Italy
Date of design: 1997

Not only is this baby's bed inspired by the
shape of an almond shell but the bed's casing
is also made from reprocessed almond shells.
The proprietary material known as Maderón is a
high-density plastic material formed by mixing
ground almond shells and other lignocellulosic
materials with natural resins and then molded.
Engineer Silio Cardona invented the process
which produces this heat-resistant, waterproof
substance. (Spain is the second biggest
harvester of almonds worldwide; the U.S.A.
is the first.)

The shape of an almond shell, the form that
inspired the cradle's casing.

The body of the crib can be used as a tub or, when the child is older, for storing toys. It
can also serve as a boat; in fact, other uses are numerous.

Water-repellent mattress and liner with
an anti-suffocating pillow.

Casing in Maderón, a non-toxic, imper-
meable, heat-insulating, transpirable,
fire-resistant (M2-class), stable material,
coated with a natural, non-toxic paint.

"Chicken legs" (four steel rods), a tribute to
Eames and a symbol of the protective hen.

Base in Maderón or beechwood.

Tamagó

Conceptual drawings by one of the designers.

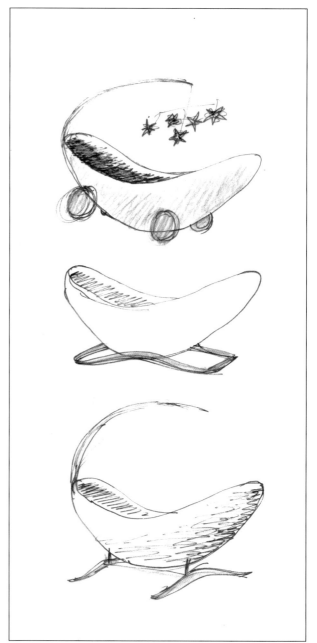

The color range with a natural-wood or painted base.

During the course of developing the Maderón casing of the cradle, a rattan version was produced as a reference to the more traditional interpretation.

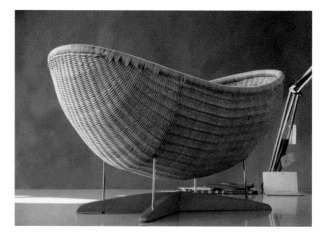

Dog Bed

Japonaise dog bed

Designer: Massimo Pelliccioni
Manufacturer: Dog Art—Magazzini Ruffi, Rome, Italy
Date of design: 1997

It may be difficult to know whether the designer and producer of this dog bed are serious. However, the fanaticism of many dog owners and their devotion to their canine companions, imbuing them with human traits, is legendary. The other 14 dog beds in the Ruffi store's range are Biedermeier, Coloniale (with a woven cane platform), Retour d'egypte (with a leather platform), Tortiglione, Barca (early 19th-century style), Luigi XIII (Louis XIII), Luigi XVI (Louis XVI), Decó (Art Déco), Romano (ancient Roman), Partenone (with Ionic columns), Baldacchino (with a canopy), Impero (Imperial Roman), Arabo (Arabic), and Viennese (Vienna Secessionist). Evidently these various styles are intended to be congruent with the décors of dog owners.

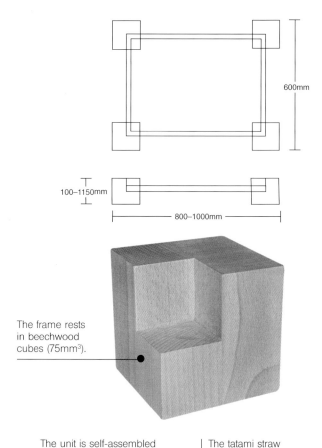

600mm

100–1150mm

800–1000mm

The frame rests in beechwood cubes (75mm^3).

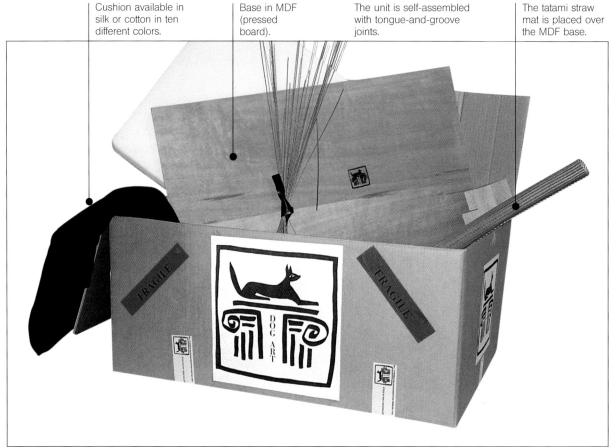

Cushion available in silk or cotton in ten different colors.

Base in MDF (pressed board).

The unit is self-assembled with tongue-and-groove joints.

The tatami straw mat is placed over the MDF base.

Designers/Manufacturers

Designers

Manufacturers